GET MEDIAWISE

WE'VE GOT NEWS FOR *YOU*

GET MEDIAWISE

WE'VE GOT NEWS FOR *YOU*

Compiled and published by:

Mediawise Communications
Oakhurst 64 Church Rd
Crown Gardens
Fleet GU3
Hampshire GU13 9PD

Telephone: 0252 622301

Book production by:
Get Mediawise: We've got news for YOU
ISBN 0-952-0405-3-0

Typesetting by **Words that Work**, Underriver, Kent
Telephone 0732 838994

Printed in Great Britain at the University Press, Cambridge

CONTENTS

Chapter 2   19
WHAT IS NEWS?

Chapter 3   45
PRESS RELEASES

Chapter 4   79
PRESS CONFERENCES

Chapter 7   161
HANDLING A MEDIA CRISIS

Chapter 8   169
APPENDIX

GET MEDIAWISE
WE'VE GOT NEWS FOR *YOU*

INTRODUCTION

Today's successful company executive will have mastered the art of communication. Unfortunately, he/she is in a minority among industrialists. It is an elite minority - but still a minority.

However, that elite band of communicators is growing in number, because the skills they possess can be taught. One channel for acquiring expertise is electronic media training. Many companies - including Mediawise Communications - will provide that.

But there is a great deal more to communication than competent performance on television or radio. To enable industrialists to command the full range of skills and so join the ranks of the elite, Mediawise Communications stands alone in offering a comprehensive media training service tailored to client needs.

Until now, no publication has drawn together the requisite threads of knowledge and practice in the art of communication. This book fills that gap.

Mediawise Communications is a media consultancy staffed by professional journalists:

- **Don Philpott** - a Fleet Street specialist in consumer affairs, food and drink for more than 20 years, and the author of many books.
- **Pam Rawlinson** - a former Fleet Street news and parliamentary reporter and sub-editor who is now administrator of Mediawise.
- **David Steers** - a Fleet Street correspondent for 17 years, a radio presenter/producer, and former joint head of public affairs of the National Farmers Union.
- **Denis Frost** - former BBC and national/regional/local newspaper correspondent and author.

This Guide covers a basic introduction to the media, press conferences and press releases, electronic media performance, crisis management, and many other areas of expertise in communication.

Get Mediawise!

The media (radio and television in particular) play an increasingly important role in our lives. We rely on them for our news, for details about what is going to happen and how it may affect our lives, and for a huge range of other information. Few of us get through a week without reading a newspaper, listening to the radio or watching television, and the impact this can have is far greater than many of us imagine.

Our attitudes and opinions are increasingly moulded by what we read in the papers, and hear and see on radio and television. Major issues are increasingly fought out in the news columns and over the air waves and, if you want to be part of that opinion forming process, you must understand how the media works, and how best to handle it. It doesn't matter if you are the press secretary of a local amateur dramatic society, or the managing director of a multinational company - the way you should deal with the media is exactly the same: you have to know **what** they want, **when** they want it, and **how** they want it. These points are dealt with briefly here, and in greater detail in their relevant chapters.

Generally speaking, you will come into contact with journalists because
(a) they want a story from you, or
(b) you have something to say to them. In either case, the result can be greatly to your advantage if you get it right, and disastrous if you get it wrong.

If a journalist contacts you, he or she is looking for information. They might be hostile, or even ask questions that you don't want to answer. Has your company, therefore, something to hide? Are the media trying to get information from you that you don't yet want published? Or is it merely an innocent inquiry as far as you can see which it will do no harm to answer? Alternatively, could this be the opening shot in a campaign which the journalist, or his or her newspaper or broadcasting organisation, wants to stir up?

"No Comment"? Never!

One of the first things you have to do is to find out exactly what the journalist in question wants from you. You should then consider the best way to respond. Whatever else you might decide is appropriate, do not answer "No comment". This can be the most damaging phrase in the English language. It immediately suggests that you have something to hide. Your job, when approached, is to help journalists and, if you can, guide them in the direction you want them to go. **Always** help journalists - as far as you are able - and, equally important, give them something to use as a "quote".

Depending on the story, you either deal with journalists yourself, or put them in touch (preferably with you as a contact) with other people in the company who know the answers or at least those answers that delineate as far as you want to go on a particular subject.

Help, Not Hinder
Make sure you provide facilities for the journalist to get at least some (if not all) of the story, and that they understand they can come back to you, or your company, at any time for clarification. Establish a procedure whereby someone is always available to speak to the journalist, and that the journalist in question has a limited set of home telephone numbers for useful company contacts. Journalists do not work office hours, and they will often want to get hold of someone in the evening, or at weekends. If your company has a proper press or public relations office, these personnel must be called in at the beginning, and armed with all the relevant facts.

Indeed, you will clearly have to tell them the full story behind whatever the problem is. There is nothing worse than a press office placed in the invidious position of trying to fend off the press when it is not in possession of the full story and background and, therefore, does not know just how far it can (or cannot) go in the comments it makes.

Again, ensure that you have experts available in the company or organisation that know the whole story, and who do not mind speaking to the press - under your supervision, of course. Always vet and approve any statements which are to be made concerning this story by any executive - including the Chairman and Managing Director. But, by and large, the easier you make the journalist's job, the more sympathetic a story you will get.

Publicity For You
If you want publicity on a particular angle of your business or achievement by your company, then you should be prepared, to some degree at least, to open your doors to the press. There are various ways of going about this. The most obvious - and often the most dangerous - is to have a press conference. It is obvious because it is an easy way of calling the press together - you can always attract some of them with just the promise of a free drink and/or a meal. It is dangerous, because a number of things can go wrong.

First, do not have a press conference unless you have something really new and different to say. Some new process or product, on its own, is not necessarily enough to get the kind of coverage you want, unless it is just a paragraph in the trade press.

Secondly, there is nothing worse than organising a press conference and then having at best only two or three journalists, and at worst no-one at all, turn up. Picture the scene: you have lined up the company chairman and the chief executive, along with a host of other experts (all of whom probably have more urgent things to do) and they find themselves faced by row upon row of empty chairs. How do you make certain that, on the one hand, you have something worthwhile to say and, on the other, that the press are interested enough to come and hear you say it?

The Successful Press Conference

There are no absolute guarantees of success, but there are ways of making your press conference an attractive and useful event.

Consider, first of all, what the journalist actually wants. First and foremost, it must be a good story, something which has not happened before, or is at least new. "First ever", "newest", "the only one of its kind" (if it really is!) - these qualities are meat and drink to the average working journalist.

The news aspect of the story is extremely important. But, by the same token, don't forget the feature writer: he will be looking for a more detailed treatment - and has more space to give you. He can go into the event in greater depth, so ensure that you have experts available who will be able to talk at length, and in layman's language, about these new developments, however technical they might be. There is, however, a down side to this tactic: the overcautious scientist who has come up with a bright idea, but hedges it around with so many "ifs", "buts" and "maybes" that the journalist is so confused he decides to forget the whole thing. Then, the effort on your part will have been a complete waste of time.

So bear this in mind: however well you try to tell your story at a press conference or a press facility visit to your company you must have a story to tell. Despite the image you may have of them, journalists are not just there for the beer.

They are spending valuable time with you because:
- they want a story
- you have promised them a story
- they have to deliver a story.

Of course they do! They are obliged to file their copy, even if only to justify the time they are spending out of the office. So if there is no story for them, you may well have prejudiced your company's entire relationship with the press, or at the very least that part of it present at the time.

iv

General Strategy

Assuming you do have a story to tell, always produce some written material, in journalistic form, which you can hand out, giving the main points of what you are trying to put across (hence the term "handout" for a press release). Further, make sure you have photographs available, either of personalities or of some specific event. They should not be what are known as "dead" pictures, featuring a manufacturing plant or a lifeless group of posed people. This kind will not be used. And remember, there is no point whatsoever in sending or giving photographs to representatives from radio stations (it's amazing how often this happens!). If the pictures are for television stations, they must be colour transparencies.

Keep speeches to the bare minimum unless you have a really exciting and *interesting* tale to tell. Do not let your technical expert drone on for half an hour on his pet subject. He may be an enthusiast, but unless he is an accomplished communicator he will bore his audience, the journalists will leave before he finishes, and there is a danger that the main point will never actually be made. **You can avoid this by incorporating the principal points of the story in the handout.**

Send out invitations at least two weeks before the event, but not a great deal earlier. It is a good idea to enclose a reply slip on the pretext of finalising your transport and catering arrangements but journalists are notoriously bad at returning these slips. Do not expect more than 30 or 40 per cent actually to reply and say they are coming. It is probably more sensible to contact invited journalists by phone a few days before the scheduled event: they'll be in a better position at that stage to give you a realistic answer. And, if some world-shattering event occurs on the day of the news conference, then you can almost guarantee that only the trade and specialist press will turn up. So plan for a 40-50 per cent attendance rate, even from the journalists who say they will come.

The following chapters explain what you should (or should not) do to get media attention and coverage, and what happens when the media come knocking at your door.

Chapter 1

GETTING TO KNOW THE MEDIA

This chapter explains the different types of media, and the choice you should make depending on the sort of information you want to publicise.

The National Press

There are 23 national daily and Sunday newspapers in Britain: their combined sale each week is a staggering 100 million copies.

At the last count there were 110 important regional morning and evening newspapers, more than 1,400 local papers, and well over 7,500 magazines and journals.

Like any other sector of retailing today, it is a very competitive market - and that is the first point to be made. Newspapers are a commodity, just like a loaf of bread or a pint of beer. If the paper does not provide consumers with what they want, it will not sell.

The tabloids, no matter what one thinks about them, have millions of readers, and the vast majority enjoy every salacious word and picture published.

People will buy a paper because they want to read it, and they would soon stop taking it if the style or content were to change significantly. Whether in good or bad taste, newspapers know what their readers want and set about providing it.

There is an old saying that "all news is good news", but this is certainly not true for newspapers.

A television newscaster attracted publicity when he called for more good news to be published and broadcast. It is not an original suggestion, and when tried in the past it has invariably failed. Newspapers which have attempted to publish only good news have quickly gone out of business. One of the leading Sunday heavies launched a good news page some years ago, but within a few issues the page had been reduced to a few paragraphs, and the idea was then dropped. At about the same time, BBC Radio started a 15-minute "good news" slot; it, too, sank without trace.

Unfortunately (or fortunately for newsmen), there is a dark side to many people to which "gloom and doom" news appeals. It is amazing, but true, that one of the biggest problems the police face when coping with a major disaster, is keeping sightseers away those looking for blood or ghoulish souvenirs from the scene. Newspapers, particularly the nationals, operate in an extremely competitive market, and they can only survive by providing what the consumer wants. We may not all like the contents and behaviour of some newspapers, but it does not bother the millions who read them.

By understanding what particular papers need, you can greatly increase the chances of getting your own stories in them. Yet there is enormous pressure for each column inch published.

Words, Words - And More Words

For example, on an average day a national "heavy" or "quality" newspaper (the Daily Telegraph, the Times, the Guardian, the Independent and the Financial Times) will have room for around 180,000 words equivalent to two and a half paperback novels. If you remove advertising and entertainment listings, there are still between 90,000 and 100,000 words of news, features, politics and sports "copy".

To supply this vast volume of material, the newspaper has its own staff reporters, specialists and subeditors; plus several hundred more "stringers" or freelance reporters working for them around the world; and the resources of the major news agencies, at home and abroad. On top of this, the newsroom is deluged daily with hundreds of press releases and handouts from public relations companies, press officers, trade organisation spokesman, Members of Parliament, charities - the list goes on and on. There are Government White Papers and reports from consumer organisations and pressure groups also competing for those precious column inches.

On heavy news days, between two and three million words of copy comes in worldwide from all these sources, of which there is room for five per cent or less. So every day, at least 1,900,000 words, and sometimes many more, are destined for the wastepaper basket. That is why it is so important when dealing with the media to get it right, and get it right first time, so that you end up in the five per cent which is used, rather than in the discarded 95 per cent.

These pressures on column inches apply right through the news gathering process. The news wire services, for instance, supply all the national newspapers with copy, but this material has first to be processed, so the final output is only a fraction of what the agency gets in.

2

The Role Of The Wire Service

The Press Association is the national news agency, and has been operating for more than 120 years. It is owned by the nation's newspapers, and does not "sell" stories but "wires them out". Each newspaper pays a subscription to belong to the "club" and, in return, receives everything sent out, to use or not, as it wishes.

At one time - not so long ago - the Press Association had 240 reporters in London, including more than 20 specialists. Every day the Press Association received up to two million words of copy from its own staff, stringers, other agencies and so on, as well as press releases, reports, books to be reviewed, and many other sources. A chunky Government White Paper or Royal Commission report alone could run to a quarter of a million words.

Each day on average, the Press Association sent out about 350,000 words to newspapers, radio and television on every subject ranging from hard news to features, parliamentary and law reports, sport, the racing results and even Court Circulars.

At any one time it has more than 11 million words stored in its computer in the form of stories and features from all the news gathering departments. This means that, at best, the Press Association was distributing only about a sixth of the copy it was sent. Today, with even greater pressure on column inches, Press Association output is even more selective, and story length correspondingly reduced.

So if a national paper uses 10,000 words of Press Association copy a day just 2+ per cent of the agency's output it can clearly be seen just how much news never makes the grade. The competition is intense, and the only way of even trying to beat the field is by learning how the newspapers work and what they want, and then tailoring your story accordingly.

Hit The Target

Only the cream of the news makes it, and the aim, when filing story ideas or press releases to any news source, is to do everything possible to maximise the chance of *your* story, and not someone else's, hitting the target. Many good stories come into newspaper offices as press releases, but for every press release that is used, at least 50 are thrown away. Press conferences can also provide journalists with hard news stories, but they often don't and are a waste of time - yours and the journalist's.

But there are other newsgenerating sources, and many stories which appear in print could never be defined as hard news - yet they obtain enormous coverage. Why? These are the offbeat articles and specialist features - and the downright silly stories, especially in the quiet weeks of summer. So a story doesn't have to be news to get into the papers, but it must be news*worthy*. Three areas are particularly important in achieving an edge over the competition:

* TARGETING   * TIMING   * HOOKS

Success in all three of these will help get your message across, and give your release that something extra which is often the difference between being used or thrown out.

Find The Right "Home"

Summing up all three targeting tasks:

1. Stories must be aimed to reach the right people.
2. They must land at just the right time.
3. There must be a hook to hang the story on - that is, it must relate to a topical event, or be a major announcement, or involve a celebrity or household name, or appear so unusual that the papers are compelled to use it.

What it comes down to is that you have to convince the journalist that your story is worth telling. This applies just as much when you are trying to get a story into the newspapers as when you are being interviewed or asked for a comment by a journalist, and want to make sure that your message is the one that gets across.

Regional Newspapers

The regional press, as opposed to the purely local press, has a unique role to play. In effect, it must perform a balancing act, or risk the danger of falling between two stools.

Its problem is that it hopes to attract readership and circulation from those people who may not take a national newspaper, but who want to know about local as well as regional and national news topics - and to see it all in one paper! This is particularly true of the regional morning newspapers, such as the Birmingham Post, Liverpool Daily Post, Yorkshire Post, and the Western Mail in Cardiff. There are several others at the moment, but these quasi-"national" regional dailies are, unhappily, a diminishing band though, oddly, they are prospering to a greater extent than local evening newspapers, many of which face extinction.

Evening Papers

Only a generation ago, most towns were served by at least two purely local weekly newspapers (usually one appearing midweek and the other on Thursday or Friday). The town would also have had access to as many as five evening papers. Certainly the London conurbation offered at that time the Star, the Evening News and the Evening Standard from London itself, plus competing regional evening papers. Each of these evening papers had its own loyal band of readers - but this was in the days before widespread television, and the Six o'clock evening news.

Nor were there many car radios then, and people who wanted to know what had happened during the day had to wait until the late news on radio the Home Service because they were not usually home in time for the early evening news. So, they bought an evening paper while out shopping, or on their way home from work, and many even had it delivered at home.

But habits changed, and radio and television took over. The casual, street corner newspaper buying habit gradually died away as news became more easily and readily available through the electronic medium. Most of the London evening papers ceased publication. The Star went first mainly because it was tied to the old News Chronicle and the other out-of-town evening papers eventually found that delivery and transport costs were just not worth the sales. Now, most towns around London get a very early edition of the only remaining London paper, the Standard, and, if they are lucky, one of the few remaining regional evening papers, together with one edition of the weekly paper. The big change has been the emergence and success of the so-called "free sheets".

However, while there is no doubt that many evening newspapers have died off, those that remain are there because they have a strong local image, and are bought by a lot of local people. Almost all of them enjoy monopoly status in the areas they serve, because they have seen off the competition. And

5

while they try to keep up with the news as it happens, they face enormous difficulties from the competition provided by radio (especially local radio) and television. So today's evening newspapers concentrate on feature material and preplanned news stories, all of which can be useful areas for you to exploit.

Copy and pictures have to be in early for editorial processing, despite the new technology and many of the stories that appear have been written the day before. Perhaps only four or five news pages are changed during the day. Frequently there are only two, or possibly three, editions of an evening paper, and some finish printing so early in the day that they have to put the four o'clock racing result in the stop press section. But they are useful vehicles for local events - and on many occasions, those papers that also own a weekly paper will channel to the weekly repeats of material which has already appeared in the evening paper, so you get two bites of the cherry.

Morning Papers

Regional morning newspapers are a different story. As outlined above, they often have great trouble in defining their optimum markets. Those with a strong local flavour, such as the Western Mail in Cardiff, try to serve the whole of Wales (they have, for instance, introduced a North Wales edition to combat the influx of the Liverpool Daily Post).

The Western Mail tends to concentrate on Welsh stories, almost to the exclusion of anything else. But many others are not so clearly defined. They want to cover local news, especially on their front pages, but they also feel they have to feature a big, and preferably sensational, national story to persuade local people to buy their paper in preference to an orthodox national morning newspaper. Of course, they do not have national correspondents except, in some cases, parliamentary and city reporters so they have to rely on the news agencies, especially the Press Association, for the coverage of national and international news. Most of the international news comes via Reuters news agency, which is housed in the same Fleet Street building as the Press Association.

Again, these newspapers are restricted by early edition times, except for late hard news, when they often put their national cousins to shame. This means that if you want space in one of these papers, in terms of keeping them informed of local and regional news, you really have to talk to their news desks the day before at the very latest. And often their features are prepared and written several days beforehand.

Regional papers do have their own specialist correspondents for many subjects and it is worth maintaining contact with these senior and respected journalists by, for example, inviting them to press conferences in London (or wherever you have your head office).

Above all, don't forget to stage the occasional (but always meaningful, in news terms) regional event during the year, when you can almost guarantee coverage in the regional and local newspapers.

The Local Press And Free Sheets

Local newspapers, surprisingly enough, can often exert more power and influence in their own areas than their national counterparts in Wapping or Fleet Street. If you misspell an MP's name in a national newspaper, nobody is likely to give it another thought; but if you get the name of a local celebrity wrong in the weekly paper, the office phone will immediately ring; there might be letters to the editor; and an apology will have to be carried when, it is hoped, they get the spelling right.

There are about 1,460 weekly newspapers in the United Kingdom, and hundreds more free sheets and "giveaways". While papers in this last category were once purely advertising vehicles, they are now competing more and more effectively with local papers (sometimes the papers that actually own them!) by carrying editorial material. In the long run, they are likely to take over from the paid weeklies in most areas, serving all the needs of the local community, and carrying a full quota of editorial and advertising -but in a newspaper distributed free of charge.

Local newspapers today are essentially a combination of the old town crier and the village gossip. The maxim that names and pictures sell papers still holds good for the weeklies, which is why so many papers continue the practice of listing all the guests at weddings and funerals, or use photographs spanning several columns portraying football teams, school classes, or the entire cast of the local amateur dramatic society's latest production. Everyone in the picture is likely to buy a copy, and possibly several more to send to friends and relatives.

Local papers do, however, have an important role to play. They are often the first channels through which local people hear news that has a direct bearing on their lives. This could be a plan for a new housing estate on your doorstep; a decision to shut down the local hospital or increase council charges; or the announcement of a new factory creating jobs and so on. People are interested in reading about things that affect them particularly; but they also want to read about people they know, whether in the context of the appearance of "Mrs X" from down the road on a shoplifting charge, or of young "Master Y" raising £5 for charity by skateboarding round the school playground. Whether we admit it or not, most of us like to gossip, or at least to listen to gossip.

The "Weeklies" - Warts And All

It might be helpful at this stage to explain how local newspapers operate. It is increasingly difficult to get a job as a trainee reporter nowadays, and most newspapers receive hundreds of applications every year for perhaps one or two vacancies. When I joined my first paper as a trainee almost 30 years ago, you had to have obtained three "A" levels, together with a certificate proving a shorthand speed of at least 60wpm.

Today the entrance requirements are even higher, and applicants are expected to master shorthand and keyboard skills quickly, to have a basic grounding in law, and a working knowledge of local government. Once accepted as a trainee, the "cub" reporter often signs articles of indentures: a three-year apprenticeship to learn the rudiments of journalism. During this time, he or she is assigned to a senior reporter, and required to attend college courses (often in another town) to learn about media law, politics and so on. At the end of the three-year training period, the junior reporter takes a proficiency examination. Unfortunately for their employers, many young journalists, on passing the proficiency test, start looking around for another job to take them a further step up the journalistic ladder.

Most young reporters want to get to the current equivalent of Fleet Street, so as soon as their indentures are completed they apply for jobs on magazines or leading regional newspapers, to gain further experience on their way to national journalism. As a result, local newspapers tend to be staffed by new trainees and senior reporters generally older people who have worked in Fleet Street or on regional papers, and who now want a quieter life, or those rare exceptions who have always been content to work in local journalism. It follows that the ratio of trainees (or those with just a few years' experience) to senior people can often be quite high.

And it is frequently the trainee's lack of experience that is responsible for the mistakes that appear in local newspapers. Some local papers do have a shocking reputation for getting the facts wrong, misspelling names, and so on, and this has even discouraged some people from providing them with stories and information. It should not, of course, because if the paper does make a mistake you can always ask for a correction in the next issue, and so get a second mention for your company. It should be noted, though, that new technology combined with a higher calibre of trainee, has led to an emphatic improvement in local press standards.

However, this is not the case if you look at local newspapers abroad. In the United States, for example, there is more than one local paper producing several editions a week and sporting a permanent "corrections" column.

But generally speaking, local papers in the United Kingdom are an excellent conduit for telling the community in which you work or operate more about yourselves. They can be used to move closer to that community and, ideally, to become an indispensable part of it. Moreover, local papers are usually very anxious for any news: if you can provide a well-written story with a good photo idea to accompany it, you should get the publicity you are seeking. The range of stories available to you is enormous. If you, or any employee of yours, have raised money for charity; won a sports event; are celebrating an anniversary, retirement or promotion; in all of these activities there is a valid human interest story which deserves to be told and should get used.

Train Your Own "Reporters"

It is important, therefore, to set up some sort of network to guarantee that stories are not missed. If you work in a public relations capacity for a company, or represent an organisation through your own consultancy, people in key positions in the company - office managers, personal assistants, union officials, anyone in the personnel department - should be asked to look out for potential stories and photo opportunities. Engage those selected in the actual process of journalism, rather in the way that weekly newspapers still appoint village correspondents who file their own distinctly amateur copy to their paper. Ask your "correspondents" to "go out and get stories" for you. It is surprising the enthusiasm which can be generated by giving people a job to do that lies outside the scope of their normal work. They can write the stories up as press releases and either channel them through you or contact the local paper themselves. If the story is big enough, the paper will simply want the facts, and will usually send its own reporter and photographer to produce the article.

> **But since many local newspapers are chronically under-staffed, it pays to find out when they have someone available to cover an event, and arrange the event to fit in with their schedule, if possible. After a little practice, your team will find that many of the stories are obvious, and score through being good news.**

Ironically, while the national newspapers do not like good news stories, the weeklies cannot print too many of them. Stories like "local boy makes good" (through a simple promotion), long service awards, a couple (retired from the company) celebrating their golden wedding anniversary - all of these make excellent local paper copy.

In a different, but equally viable, category come the corporate stories of, for instance, plans to create new jobs, or the company report announcing a record year's trading: the currency here is wider, because the Financial Times and the city pages of the quality nationals will also be interested. But don't neglect local paper interests either: avoid giving the impression that you are feeding the local outlet only the "bread and butter" stories; treat every outlet alike with the more marketable information. And, in general, operate on the thesis that there is a story to be had in almost anything.

There was a famous regional news editor, a dour Cornishman who had trained on the Falmouth Packet, one of the great names in local newspapers, who used to say "Don't come back to the office till you have got a story". He would never ever accept the argument that there just wasn't a story in the event to which you had been sent. He was right: and very often the story the reporter came back with was not the one he/she had been sent out to get! Local papers don't "dump" stories on the scale that national papers do.

While the nationals are under tremendous pressure with the avalanche of copy they have to deal with, this is rarely the case with weekly newspapers. There is a tale - no doubt apocryphal - of a young local paper reporter sent to cover the opening of a new community centre by the mayor. A couple of hours later the news editor spotted the reporter back behind his desk - yet no story had been filed. "Where's the copy about the opening?", asked the news editor. "Oh, there's no story", replied the young reporter, blandly. "The opening was cancelled because the community centre had burned down during the night!" It may be a silly story but it does illustrate that all too often even the professionals can see only one story when an even bigger one is staring them in the face.

But apart from getting stories in the local newspaper - which all companies and organisations should try to do either for public relations or commercial advantage - it is vital to cultivate a good working relationship with the local paper and its representatives, from the editor down. The chances are that in a small community, the local bank manager, leading shopkeepers and employers, top officials of clubs and societies and so on, will know the editor and the senior reporters. Almost without exception, these personal contacts can be worth their weight in gold. The "old boys' network" is extraordinarily active in the local community.

Equally, it is obviously worth cultivating journalists who specialise in your areas of business. It is always better, when faced with a difficult situation, to be able to ring up a journalist you have met, who knows you and, more important, can trust you. If you have that kind of relationship with a reliable local news source, you stand a greater chance of influencing how a story will appear in print. Like the chairman of the council, and a grammar school headmaster, the local journalist is a big fish, albeit in a small pond. Journalists can exert enormous influence and they make much better allies than enemies.

The Free Sheets

Love them or hate them, free sheets can, in many circumstances, provide good coverage of your particular subject, but often with the proviso that you back up editorial space with advertising. Opinions are divided on whether people actually read free newspapers. They are pushed through your letterbox whether you have asked for them or not, and distribution can be very patchy - you may get a free sheet one week but not the next, because of problems with deliverers. The quality of coverage of local events is extremely variable: some are very good, but others print only a token amount of editorial matter. There are people who regard free sheets as junk mail and refuse to have them delivered at all, or discard them unseen as soon as they drop through the letterbox. However, others - and they are the huge majority - take full advantage of the advertising services the free sheets offer to dispose of unwanted items and acquire others.

Yet a good free sheet can be useful, particularly for feature articles. They all have small staffs, and anyone who can provide good copy can almost guarantee getting space; but you will inevitably get a call from the advertising department asking you to take paid space as well.

Advertising: The Key

The livelihood of all newspapers depends on advertising. It is advertising, not the cover price, that pays the wages and the rates. And, in the case of the free papers, advertising is everything. If they could achieve that sort of split, all newspapers would love to work on a ratio of 40:60 editorial to advertising. Most settle happily for 50:50, and are lucky if they can reach that mark. **In the case of the free sheets, they are often working towards a 90:10 breakdown - with the 90 per cent being advertising!** Rather than aim for increased editorial space, which is costly, a newspaper will quickly reduce the number of pages if advertising falls off.

Both local and free papers (indeed, all newspapers) love pictures. People are generally vain, and if their photograph appears in a newspaper, they normally place multiple orders, both of the paper and the pictures. Photographs, in other words, guarantee sales and revenue. So there are many opportunities for offering your own pictures new appointments, retirements, special offbeat events, firm's sports day, society's annual dinner, WI sale, etc - especially if they all show lots of faces!

But remember, there are two ways of photographing an event: the right and the wrong way. This is discussed in more detail in Chapter 3.

Specialist Press

The world of specialist magazines has to be divided into those serving the trade and those serving the consumer, because each has a quite separate function to fulfil. The trade press can, again, be subdivided into those journals which simply reproduce virtually all handouts sent to them, and those which do exercise editorial control over content, and develop their own stories. You can quickly determine into which categories the various trade magazines and papers fall.

The purpose of a press release is to inform, and if trade magazines carry press releases in full, which are read by the audience for which they were written, then a useful role has been played. After all, that is what the publicity game is all about getting stories into newspapers and magazines. There is the question, however, of credibility. Does an article written by a staff or accredited freelance journalist have more credibility than an obvious press release, even though both contain exactly the same information?

In a recent survey, a large percentage of readers admitted that they were unable to distinguish between editorials and "advertorials" (paid-for space combining editorial and advertising elements). However, of those who claimed they could tell the difference, fewer than a third said the information in advertorials could be trusted, and more than 40 per cent thought the information was less convincing than in editorial copy. The trade press is a crucial media sector to target. Trade papers have an enormous appetite for specialist news and, usually, much more space available to devote to it. An item which merits only a paragraph in a regional newspaper might make a double-page feature in a specialist trade magazine.

So try to find out the sort of stories and features the specialist magazines like to cover; the style in which they write them; the kind of photographs, illustrations and graphs they like to use; and, particularly, the specialist areas of journalists on the staff. Again, if you have a good story your chances of getting it used are greatly increased if you channel it to the person on the magazine who actually covers that specialist area, and is thus most likely to appreciate its newsworthiness.

The Electronic Media

As distinct from the print media, the electronic media now exist at every level of our lives. Daily, and for 24 hours a day in some cases, television and radio count their audiences in tens of millions.

The important thing for you is that each medium especially radio, since there is so much more of it has a voracious appetite for topical material; usually, this is to service current affairs programmes or news bulletins.

National broadcasting by radio and television is networked to the nation either by the BBC or by the commercial companies currently licensed and regulated by the Independent Television Commission (ITC) and the Radio Authority. There are also BBC regional television outposts in most of the major cities, plus a number of satellite stations, supplying their own areas and backing up the "headquarters" broadcasting from London.

At the time of writing, there were two terrestrial (land-based) BBC channels transmitting from London, and two commercial channels. Their ITV counterparts also operate on a regional basis, sometimes in harness - as, for example, Carlton and LWT sharing the London area.

On the radio side, the BBC transmits from London and its important regional centres, which broadcast independent services as well as feeding the national networks at Broadcasting House and Bush House, home of the External Services. Commercial radio has one big London station (the franchise changed hands in 1993) providing a national and international news service to the network. In addition to the BBC's (currently) five domestic channels, and the World Service, there are already nearly 200

BBC, independent and community local radio stations - and the number is growing all the time.

The BBC's national radio monopoly now has opposition from nationwide commercial channels - the classical music channel, Classic FM, and Virgin 1215AM - doing roughly the same job as BBC Radio 3 and Radio 1.

The position with television satellite broadcasting is fluid, and will continue to be so. People in the United Kingdom with the correct equipment, cable service and decoders can now receive up to 20 popular satellite channels - a situation that would have been unbelievable ten years previously. The prime mover for the foreseeable future is likely to be Rupert Murdoch's News International organisation, through Sky Television. But the excellent global news service, CNN, is also widely seen in the United Kingdom.

Local broadcasting - both radio and television - serves, at the moment, a defined geographical area bounded by transmitter reach.

That is the general picture of a multiplicity of services which, in our leisure hours, are regarded as a family friend and provider of entertainment and release, while, in our professional lives, they too often take on the character of "the enemy" - or to some at least, the journalists who staff the media assume that character.

This designation is, of course, unfair. A journalist is the enemy only of people, interests, factions or concerns which are seeking to conceal the truth. That there are exceptions to this generalisation serves only to validate the truth. The customary demand of a journalist is, as we have noted, for just one thing, a good story. Reporters rarely possess other than a superficial knowledge of any subject, unless they're specialists, in which case they are correspondents in a limited range of activity. They have their own contacts, and if a Government department or an industry or lobby wishes to pass information or simply to get publicity, then it is invariably to the correspondent or to his news desk that they will turn.

This is the person whom they know and whom, in most cases, they can trust. A correspondent cannot afford to alienate a good contact. Unfortunately, the contact, especially if he or she is part of the Whitehall publicity machine, can sometimes, unwillingly betray the correspondent. Then a relationship which is, admittedly, very often open to corruption, breaks down: though generally not for long.

But the reporter chasing a topical news story will want only the germane facts and as quickly as possible. So reporters must turn to people having a greater acquaintance with, or awareness of, the subject matter. A reporter will generally approach you for what you know, not for what you think.

If, on the other hand, the media regularly asks you for your opinion, this is not necessarily flattering. It could mean no more than that you are known for being splendidly indiscreet - a source of good quotes or, even worse (for example, like some backbench MPs) that you are willing to perform by endorsing any opinion, however bizarre, at any hour of the day or night. This armour, of the reliable controversialist, is frequently worn by those whose political careers are beyond any hope of resurrection.

So let us assume that a story has broken involving your industry to which you are a central source, both as a provider of fact and opinion in the form of reaction. For one thing, the varying forms of story treatment will dictate differing responses from you.

Bulletins And Programmes

The shortest type of reaction is clearly the news bulletin, on television and radio. The essence of a news bulletin is brevity: in the British media, no news bulletin (with the exception of Channel Four News) lasts for more than half an hour, and a great many are summaries taking up no longer than a minute or two of air time. The news bulletin is totally unlike a newspaper in its treatment of news. In the electronic media, the newscaster or newsreader establishes the basic facts of the story from a prepared script. What, for a newspaperman, would be his first and most important paragraph - the "who, what, where, when and why" - is, in a television or radio bulletin, not the province of the reporter at all. It forms the cue material, which the correspondent will then elaborate and illustrate.

For this entire process of telling the story, the bulletin reporter rarely has more than a minute of air time. Television and radio journalists tend to speak at about three words a second, so that's 180 words say, 15 or 16 lines, doublespaced, on an A4 sheet of paper. With the "lead" story of the day there is a bit more flexibility but not much. And in most cases, the story will be supported by what the trade calls "actuality" - related film or wildtrack sound; or, more often, an extract from an interview.

The "Sound Bite"

In the case of radio (and sometimes of television) the full interview will be used in current affairs or magazine programmes, with the news bulletin carrying what is known as a "clip" - or increasingly, following the more colourful American designation, a "sound bite". It follows then, that the sound bite must be lucid and trenchant. This is the "instant quote", the encapsulation of what you want to say if you are going to make the headlines. And you have to be able to say it in, preferably, under 20 seconds.

No matter how long the interview goes on, what the news bulletin wants is a clip: the reporter or correspondent will isolate the clip, and a film, video or magnetic tape editor will extract it. But if the material for the sound bite isn't there, then it won't be **you** on the Nine O'Clock News or News at Ten, but somebody else who **has** provided the perfect sound bite. It takes practice to get the clip right, but it is well worth the effort.

It also takes intensive media training, as any professional communicator - MP, industrialist or entertainer - will readily acknowledge. Some people, who are accomplished tacticians in dealing with the press, can manipulate the sound bite factor to alarmingly good effect. Indeed, it is by no means far-fetched to say that American general elections are won or lost on the battle of the sound bites. What the viewer sees and hears on the evening news bulletin, which then passes to the daily newspapers the following morning, is what the potential voter remembers when he enters the polling centre.

When Harold Wilson was Prime Minister and making a speech to, for example, his party conference, he had a way of conveying the imminence of the clip - a certain look or gesture to the cameras, even a prearranged signal, to make sure they were rolling - with, of course, the tacit implication that as far as the news bulletins were concerned, they could forget about the rest of the speech, because the clip was there, and that is all they would need. News management? Naturally, but it saved valuable time for the news outlet, and it is a lesson that politicians and most others who regularly appear on the radio and television have quickly grasped.

What it comes down to is this: if you're giving the keynote address at a conference or at an important seminar, and you want publicity, then you have two distinct audiences: the one you're talking to in the hall, and the one outside that you can't see.

You have to speak to both, and make sure both hear your messages.

The Interview

Having mastered the art of the sound bite you still have to cope with the interview as a whole. The interview is the vital ingredient of current affairs programmes, which themselves occur at all times of the day on domestic television and radio and, in the BBC World Service, throughout the night. Current affairs programmes do more than extend and analyse the news: they reflect the life and the character of the nation or community as well.

Programme formats vary, but the basic ingredients are a mix of hard news and features, relying strongly on interviews. And whatever sort of show it is - local, regional or national; "chat"-or discbased; consumer or specialist-oriented - a current affairs programme provides the person seeking publicity with a very useful forum or platform.

In normal circumstances, you'll have nothing to fear from the broadcast interview. If it is a live interview, you will obviously have a measure of control; if it is recorded, the words that come out at the other end are still going to be yours.

Yes, it is possible to cut and rearrange sentences, words, even syllables, but the purpose of editing a radio or television interview is invariably to remove chunks of matter so that the remainder can be fitted into the required timespan; nothing more than that. No broadcasting outlet with any sense of responsibility or awareness of the legal implications is deliberately going to engineer statements that were never made. Of that you can be sure: in editing a tape or film, the programme may well leave out something you wanted kept in but you have no control over that. Editorial control belongs to the broadcasters: the ultimate sanction which you have is that you can forbid the interview being broadcast at all. Bear in mind though, that if you do this, it is almost certain that you will never be asked to appear again.

With the live interview, unless you're an actual or suspected criminal, or a politician or, as is sometimes the case, both -the interviewer, ie, the presenter of the programme, is not attempting to trap you or make you look ridiculous, or destroy your reputation.

The programme, like the reporter, is interested only in ascertaining the relevant facts or opinions. On the other hand, if you give the impression that you have got something to hide, then you must expect to be asked about it. Or if the story depends on your being frank and truthful, and you are patently neither, the person on the other side of the studio is going to point this out, gently or otherwise.

There are rare exceptions: the presenter who feels he or she has a name to make as an incipient Jeremy Paxman or Jon Snow. The most you can end up with is the sympathy vote of the watching or listening audience when the presenter as local presenters frequently do oversteps the mark.

Or there is the subject matter: child cruelty, animal welfare, racial prejudice are strong examples where the presenter might feel that no bounds of decency or good manners need to be observed. You can then, if you feel sufficiently aggrieved, walk out.

But whatever the subject of the interview, there are some ground rules which you should always follow. These are dealt with in much greater detail

17

in Chapter 5, but if you are offered an interview, by all means accept the opportunity, though you must make sure that:

- **You are the right person to talk about the subject**
- **You have enough time to marshal your thoughts and research your material.**

So ask the producer of the programme for specific briefings on the subject for interview, the degree of detail required, the type of programme and audience, the duration of the interview and, obviously, whether it's to be "live" or recorded, and the content of at least the first question. Even at the risk of making a nuisance of yourself, try to get these points clear in your mind.

Learn your brief; whatever else you do, never go into the studio unprepared. And when the time comes, make the points you want to make, regardless of the questions you're asked. There are courteous ways of doing this.

To be a good interviewee you must be willing. Most people are nervous at the thought of being interviewed, but if you know your subject you shouldn't have anything to worry about.

If the interviewee is ill-prepared and ill-fitted for the role he/she has taken on, it will soon become glaringly obvious and an embarrassment. And, above all, a fantastic opportunity to get your message across to a huge audience will have been wasted.

Interview strategy and techniques, illustrated by actual and theoretical examples of the art of the interview, are fully explained in Chapter 6.

Chapter 2
THE NATURE OF NEWS

There are different sorts of news: hard news, offbeat news, and feature material. It is a fallacy to believe that your newspaper carries all the major news stories every day. You have only to compare the front page headlines of different newspapers each day to see that this isn't the case. All the papers may choose different lead stories, and some may not even mention stories at all which others considered lead material.

The newspapers provide a snapshot of what has taken place in the previous 24 hours and, while most of the main stories will be covered, far more news stories are omitted than published. The situation is even tighter on radio and television where only the main stories are used in news bulletins. People don't like their papers filled with downbeat material, so silly stories, offbeat stories and features are used to provide a balance and to delve into subjects in more depth. Most inside pages are largely made up with "soft" news. These stories usually have the added advantage of being relatively timeless, so they can be slotted into the paper on any day over a given period. They normally concern offbeat incidents or "amazing" facts, but their common ingredients constitute the sort of story which that particular paper likes to carry.

All papers have a different style, and areas of special interest. To improve the chances of a press release or a tipoff about a story finding a home, you must endeavour to provide the paper with the sort of story you know it prefers, ideally written in a style similar to the one it uses. If you can provide a really interesting or offbeat story, as near to the house style as possible and at the right time you will maximise its potential.

Timing is important, because there is no point in sending a story or press release to a newspaper as it is about to go to press (or, indeed, *after* it has gone to press!). If you think you have a good inside page story to tell, try to find out when the paper's sub-editors start to lay out the inside pages. The times will vary, depending on whether it is a morning or evening paper, or a weekly publication. If your story is newsworthy and lands in the newspaper office just as they are about to make the pages up, it is much more likely to be used than if it arrives late, with perhaps four or five stories left but only one gap in the page to fill.

There is no reason why your news release shouldn't be presented as a news story, **but it must have real impact.** It has to be a story worth carrying - although, as we have already said, this doesn't necessarily mean that it must be hard news. But still, it should be something the readers will want to look at. That is one reason why offbeat stories always do so well. People enjoy reading about the silly things other people get up to.

Off-beat stories could relate to a new product, or a "coals to Newcastle" export order; they could describe a novel way of raising money for charity; or feature a former pupil at the local secondary school who has come back as headmaster. It doesn't really matter what the subject is, provided it is something that interests the reader.

Some stories are almost hardy annuals: the "Glorious Twelfth" (the start of the grouse-hunting season); the Beaujolais Nouveau wine race; the cost of strawberries on the first day of Wimbledon; and so on. Thanks to the speed of telecommunications today, there is even a new media phenomenon: the boomerang story.

An enterprising local paper reporter might hear an interesting story on the local radio news bulletin. The reporter checks it out (usually), scribbles down a few paragraphs and phones the story to the national news agency, the Press Association. The Press Association then sends it out over the wire to all national and regional newspapers, as well as radio and television stations. It is not uncommon for the local radio station which first carried the story to pick it up again and use it in a bulletin! In this way, a story can sometimes do the rounds for several days, often becoming embroidered in the process.

So news doesn't have to be news to make the newspapers, but it does have to be newsworthy. Above all, stories must help to sell the newspaper. Newspapers are a commodity which the public can choose to buy as they wish.

Every paper knows exactly what its readers want and expect. It is an interesting exercise to buy all the national newspapers one day, and compare how each has treated the same story. A recent story involving a major city fraud was covered by all the national newspapers, "heavies" and tabloids. The amount of money involved in the fraud, depending on which paper you read, ranged from £20 million to £60 million. Even when the source of the story is a news agency report, and all the papers receive the same material over the wire, the interpretation and handling of the story can vary enormously from paper to paper.

For example, the fact that Britain is one of the most sober nations in the world (we are actually drinking less than we did ten years ago) does not make good headline material in the popular press - yet the activities of a small minority of "lager louts" will command a disproportionate amount of space.

It is a sad but time-honoured truism that stories of catastrophe, shock statistics and frightening events do get a lot of exposure. The material on which these stories are based is frequently drawn from responsible reports, but these sources tend to constitute only a small element of the overall picture. It is generally a question of selective emphasis: a reported statistic proving that 95 per cent of the population does not have a criminal record is impressive in itself, but perhaps not persuasive enough for the popular papers. However, employing the same statistic but turning it round so that it now reads "One in 20 people has criminal record", and you have a headline that really, as far as many newspapers are concerned, hits the spot.

DEALING WITH THE MEDIA

The Approach - And How To Handle It

Dealing with the media really boils down to two situations: either you approach the media or it approaches you.

Let us begin with the latter case. A journalist is chasing you for a statement or comment about something your company has done, is doing, or plans to do. It could concern a new product, or some other commercially sensitive matter; an industrial dispute, a redundancy plan or a workforce relocation scheme - in other words, you may not necessarily want to make a comment about it. However, it could transpire that the journalist wasn't looking for a reaction from you which directly affected either you or your company at all. It may simply be that you have developed a reputation as an expert in a certain field, so the reporter is seeking a comment or reaction to some news event like the publication of a government or local authority report on a matter affecting industry or politics in a more general way.

So you may have been chosen because yours is a leading company in the field, or you have a good export record - or simply because the news outlet knows you are good for a "quote". But the reporter will scarcely ever have picked your name at random. There will be a reason why you in particular were selected: the most likely is that the contact you have developed with

21

the media has lodged you firmly in the filing systems of Fleet Street and the electronic outlets. They know who you are and what you do...and they also know that you are invariably available for comment if required.

THE NEWSPAPER TELEPHONE INTERVIEW

Points to watch

Try to determine how much the journalist actually knows about the story concerning your company or organisation.

Give him/her the background from your point of view, possibly in these terms: "I'm not sure how much you know, but...."

It is also worth checking whether the interview is being tape-recorded by the newspaper. This is an increasingly common practice; in theory the reporter should tell you, but in any event you ought to ask.

If you are unsure about the reporter's credentials, take a name and phone number and call the office back - though he may be freelance working on a story that has not yet been offered to a particular outlet. Even so the paper will know him.

Never be trapped into saying something you don't mean. An interviewer will frequently give you a long statement of the facts of a story as they are currently known, adding "Do you agree with that?" If you then answer "Yes" it will be taken to mean that you have lent your name to the entire statement in every detail.

Other questions which should arouse suspicion are those starting "Isn't it true that...? or "I've been told that your company has..." or "Rumour has it that...". Always be on your guard with this approach: request clarification or substantiation of the "rumour", and use the "pregnant pause" or simply give a noncommittal answer..."Oh?" or "Really?" or "I haven't heard that".

When you have given a reporter an important quote or complicated answer, you would be well advised to ask him to read it back to you for checking.

You can always request a newspaper to read a story over to you before it is printed: many will not do this, but some readily agree, so it is worth the effort.

Be consistent. In a major running story you will be approached by several journalists, all asking the same questions. It is important that you should make the same points to each, and try not to become bored, and therefore careless, because you are simply repeating an identical message nine or ten times. Remember that each reporter is hearing what you have to say for the first time.

It is not unknown for a newspaper to have several reporters working on the same story. Two, or even three, might deliberately phone you putting the same points, to see if you can be persuaded to change your story.

Equally, it is essential that every person representing the company or organisation to the press speaks with a common voice.

THE NEWSPAPER FACE-TO-FACE INTERVIEW

Don't keep journalists waiting: power-play one-upmanship doesn't work.

Normal rules of hospitality apply: offer refreshments if appropriate.

Make sure you are not disturbed by incoming phone calls or other interruptions.

Come out from behind your big desk, and sit facing each other in comfortable chairs - but provide the journalist with a flat surface on which to rest his notebook.

It is common practice for a journalist to keep a miniature tape recorder running during an interview, in addition to taking notes. Tape recorders are now small enough to be concealed in the top pocket of a coat and still make a perfect recording. A directional microphone can be hidden inside a pen, or a video camera in a briefcase. Why not take a leaf out of their book - and also guard against being misquoted - by having your own tape recorder running.

Never assume that the interview is over even if the recorder is switched off, or the notebook closed. Act on the assumption that nothing is "off the record", whatever assurances you might have received.

The onus is upon you to get the message across. If you are not asked the appropriate questions, you must still ensure that you make the right points.

Keep cool and collected: never lose your temper with either the journalist or the line of questioning.

When you feel the questioning has gone far enough, politely terminate the interview.

Developing Contacts

This is a two way trade, and worth cultivating. If you are likely to come into contact with the media on a regular basis, it is worth taking the time and effort to get to know key journalists. As, for instance, press officer for the local amateur dramatic society, you should be on familiar terms with the local paper's show business or entertainments writers - and their second strings, who stand in for them when are on holiday. If you are in business, you must meet the specialists on the city and business pages. You will find this mutually beneficial - and it could perform a useful service for you in persuading you not to underestimate these local or regional reporters, correspondents and critics. They wield significant power and, almost without exception, use it fairly and wisely.

The shopworn and outdated image of journalists staggering back to the office after a long, liquid lunch has given way to a very different reality. Pressures created by advanced technology have resulted in journalists now spending less time out of the office and more at the computer terminal. So if you want to introduce yourself to a journalist, try to arrange a quick chat over a coffee or drink somewhere close to his/her office.

Most journalists will agree to a brief meeting just to see who you are and how useful you might be in the future. Make sure you use that time effectively to explain what you do, what your plans are, and how you can be useful to the news outlets. Give the reporter your office desk number and home telephone number as a sign of mutual trust. It is unlikely you will get the journalist's home telephone number in return at this early stage, but there are professional reasons for this. Many journalists and news desks refuse to give out home telephone numbers to protect their staff against improper pressure. For example, a reporter covering a court case will not want phone calls to his home suggesting, in no uncertain terms, what he should and should not report.

But if you develop a rapport with a journalist and can prove that you are a good source of stories and information, you will be given his home number, if only in the hope of a story to scoop his colleagues or the opposition. Study the media's needs: are they planning special features in which you, your company or society could have an input? Is there a supplement which might feature your organisation, or a forthcoming news event coming up to which you can alert the journalist, or simply a good photo opportunity? Once you have established that contact, it is worth developing. But try not to be too pushy, or waste their time with corporate "puffs". Be fair and straightforward, so that when you do make contact, they know that you will have something they can use.

While trust is the essential ingredient in developing really good media contacts, never take anything for granted. Many journalists would happily sell their grandmothers for a major scoop, and pledges like "off the record" are, in some circumstances, not likely to be honoured. So until you know how far your media contacts can be wholly trusted, tread carefully. If you have invited a reporter to your office, make sure there are no sensitive or confidential documents on view. Journalists are adept at reading upside down, and most have a third ear which is able to home in on other conversations in the vicinity. Never assume, because a journalist has put his notebook away, that anything you say after that is off the record and will not be used. The very act of closing the notebook might have been a deliberate ploy to get you to open up.

The "Other" Editors

The Editor is, naturally, the senior journalist, and ultimate editorial authority, on any newspaper. He or she will be an invaluable contact for you - but, if they know their job, editors will rarely rarely permit close relationships with leading members of their community who are not already close friends. An editor simply cannot afford to cultivate friendships with people who might then misuse that relationship to exert improper pressure on him. By all means strike up an acquaintance with the editor of the paper that serves your area of interest; but your best interests are more likely to be served by cultivating the important departmental heads - the News Editor, Diary Editor, Picture Editor, Features Editor and, on a morning paper, the Night Editor.

The features pages provide all manner of opportunities on which you might capitalise, and can offer far more space than the news pages to get your message across. Because feature articles consist of large blocks of words, they look better if the text is broken up with pictures or other illustrations, so again, they will take most if not all of the appropriate photographs you supply.

However, the News Editor is the senior journalist as far as day-to-day running of the news floor is concerned. Ultimately it is the News Editor who decides which jobs are covered and which are not; which stories are to be built up, and followed up. If you have a complaint against a newspaper because of a misleading article, or any other problem, it is the News Editor who is normally responsible for resolving it, even if initially you took your complaint directly to the Editor.

The Picture Editor is responsible for allocating jobs to photographers and, often, for selecting photographs for publication as well. Finally, the Diary Editor (usually called Forward Planning Editor in broadcasting) is a natural target for a determined publicist. The Diary Editor keeps the news diary up-to-date - not just events happening in the next few days, but even months and years ahead. The Diary Editor can normally tell you if the event you are planning is likely to clash with anything else, or if there is something else happening of which you might be able to take advantage.

If you have a project in mind for which you want maximum publicity, the Diary Editor is your first priority, followed by the Picture Editor: they "pencil you in" the diary and inform you what the news opposition to your story is likely to be. Nearer the date you will provide the news desk with a more detailed programme so that the paper can assess the strength of the story in the light of other events of that day, and prepare a team to cover it. A timetable is invaluable: a reporter - and certainly a photographer - cannot afford to sit around for hours on end waiting for the kernel of the story, and the picture opportunity, to emerge. Help the paper's executives all you can: they will be duly grateful, and you will see the results in the following day's/ week's edition.

Using Your Contacts

A responsible journalist who is grateful for the relationship you are trying to establish with him will not expect to be fed stories from the first time you meet. It is, therefore, a rewarding strategy to make the initial contact at a "soft" event - your annual dinner, say, or the directors' lunch following the annual meeting of your company. It is a bonus for the reporter if you have a VIP after-dinner speaker, or if an actual news line emerges from the meeting in the shape of a human interest angle or a revealing announcement. To put yourself further in credit without compromising your own or your company's position, ensure that the journalist is given red carpet treatment. If the VIPs are treated to predinner drinks in a separate room away from the other guests, make sure the journalist is invited to join them. It will flatter the journalist, and cost you nothing. It is also a good idea to designate someone to "chaperone" each member of the press, not only to make them feel at home, but to keep a close check on their activities as well.

Good media contacts are imperative to a company's public image. If a major story is about to break in your area, a journalist contact may well ring you first for your comment or reaction. This could be hugely important to you by providing a vital early warning. Should the story be hostile, directly involving you, your company or organisation, that warning might permit you to get your side of events over, and correct any misleading allegations opponents have thrown at you.

On no account should you ever attempt to suppress a story -you will, in any case, not be able to; but with the extra time you have gained, you can score heavily in damage limitation simply by controlling the flow of information to the media. And, if the unwelcome story is also blatantly untrue, it is better that your reporter contact discovers this now, than after it has appeared in print. A responsible newspaper will not publish an item it knows to be untrue, but if damaging material does get into print because you have refused to co-operate or even comment, then no matter how innocent you or your company are in the matter, some mud will inevitably stick, especially if you have been worked over by one of the tabloids.

And even if, in the last analysis, you cannot prevent a prejudicial story from appearing, that early warning will have given you at least an opportunity of preparing and issuing a holding statement, which is always better than "no comment". A holding statement as bland as: "The matter is under discussion at this moment and it is hoped to issue a full statement shortly", is still preferable to silence, which can serve only to increase the burden of suspicion on you.

If nothing else, it suggests that something is being done, and holds out the promise that more will follow later, although the press cannot hold you to this as you deliberately said "it is hoped to issue...."

Alternatively - and this will not surprise the press - you can adopt the camouflaged language of Whitehall.

If a ministerial spokesperson describes a story as "pure speculation", this can be taken to mean "it's absolutely true, but it's premature to say so". A total distortion of the facts" really means "you're basically right, but you've got one or two points wrong so we can go on denying it for a little while longer". "No decision has yet been taken" indicates that a decision has been made, but the Whitehall mandarins have not yet told the Minister about it.

Government departments can get away with this sort of subterfuge because, while they have large information departments to do their bidding, the basic function of a Department of State is not, as such, to keep the press informed. The press are told only what the Department decides it is politically expedient that they should be told; anything else is denied them - or simply denied.

Sometimes a Government press officer can truthfully say that his department has no idea whether a leaked report is true because they have genuinely not been told about it - although his *minister* knows. At other times, the press office *will* know about the leak but they have been instructed, for whatever reason, not to reveal it to the press. Of course, you cannot get away with that in the private sector - at least, not more than once.

One of the best ways of losing a press contact is to sell a journalist a dud story - or, even worse, to pass on something you know to be untrue, but which could give you an edge, commercial or otherwise. Most of the queries a journalist will put to you can be easily fielded at no cost to you or your company. They may even result in beneficial publicity - and that is what media relations are all about.

Tactical Approaches

Use the telephone. If you send out a press release, it might easily be thrown away unread, intentionally or otherwise. So confirm receipt by phone. The journalist you speak to may not have seen your press release, but you can persuade him that the story is still worth telling. If you have invited a newspaper or a particular correspondent to an event and have not received a reply, phone them and ask if someone is coming. It is often more difficult for the news outlet to say "no" on the telephone, and if you get through to a named person on the news desk, you have made another contact who could be useful on another occasion.

Handling the media in an emergency or crisis situation requires a different, specialist approach, which is dealt with in Chapter 7. What you should aim at within your company or organisation is to make someone responsible at all times for taking press inquiries. This is not a "nine-to-five" job confined cosily within office hours. A journalist is just as likely to ask you for a statement at 7pm (if he works for a morning paper), as he is at 7am (if he's on an evening paper) or on a holiday weekend Saturday if he is a Sunday paper man. News is a round-the-clock, seven-days-a-week business, and somebody in the company - or, preferably, a team to ensure blanket coverage - has to be available to answer press calls.

An almost unbelievable situation happened a few years ago, when there was a total stoppage at all United Kingdom plants of a major motor company. The company were unable to field a single trained spokesperson and, for the first few days of a damaging dispute, the sole official voice of the company was a press officer flown in from a plant on the continent. At times it was difficult to understand his English, but he was the only person the company allowed to talk: the result was that in the propoganda war being fought on the television screens, the union won hands down.

Remember: if you or your organisation are going to be in touch with the media on a regular basis, you need to field someone who is competent to do it.

This involves recognising media opportunities and deriving the optimum benefit from them. You not only have to know what makes a good story: you must develop a sense of timing, so that when the story is released to the press it gains maximum impact for the company. The way to generate the type of story the press wants to publish is either to create them yourself, or form a network within your company which will provide you with information so that you can assess it for news value.

Company Networks

You may find that one piece of information in isolation from one source may not in itself be significant, but if you are given several items from a number of sources, you might realise that it is possible to weld them together in such a way that you *do* have a good story. For instance, a modest export order from a company with several divisions may not be newsworthy, but if

29

several divisions report orders, then it *is* worth a story. One man in a factory winning a prize in a competition is not particularly stunning: five workers winning prizes in different competitions is, however, a good offbeat story. Although the story is notionally about luck in competition entries, it does give you the opportunity to plug the fact that they all work for your company. You could even arrange for the winners to be photographed at work, so that the company name appears in the background.

In the same way, one office girl getting married is news only for the weddings page in the local weekly. But if two or even three girls, all from the same office, are getting married on the same day, that could make the general news pages. Most run-of-the-mill news stories present themselves, but you should take advantage of them if you can. However, you will always look for the offbeat story, and try to dig out your own "scoops". After all, a reporter is only as good as his sources, and if you have good lines of communication through your organisation, you should pick up all sorts of intelligence, some of which will almost certainly form the basis of news copy. The secret is being able to recognise what makes a good story.

TOPICAL TIPS

Timing can be critical in determining whether your story or news release is published. It has to be sent in early enough for it to be subbed and get in the paper, but you must always weigh up carefully how "time-sensitive" the story is. Clearly, an item relating to a football match or a wedding is not much use to the paper if you file it several days after the event. But there are all manner of stories which stand a better chance of making it into print if you time their release correctly. Saturday newspapers, for instance, are usually thinner than on weekdays, and contain more features and sports pages, so the space available for news is correspondingly smaller. Monday morning papers, however, don't have any court cases to report, or proceedings in parliament, and may have more space available. If you have a news story which is not so time-sensitive, it is, therefore, better to target it for a Monday than a Saturday. Other factors come into play as well, and it is trying to best-guess all of them and act on this information that is going to give you the greatest chance of getting your news published.

> **A few more points to bear in mind:**
> - Papers are normally thinner during August when many people are on holiday
> - There is generally a lesser news flow on the day following a Bank Holiday, or just after Christmas
> - Study your own local newspapers - you may spot other quiet news days, and take advantage of them.

A phone call to a journalist giving the relevant information could be all that is needed to trigger publication or broadcasting of a story. Or you might strike lucky with a press release: if it is properly written and sets out all the facts, then it will give the journalist all the information he/she needs to write the story.

Pick the right angle to appeal to the reporter and the story will appear in the paper in the way that reflects best on your company. You may, on the other hand, feel that a press conference is the best way to get your message over. All these approaches incorporate advantages and disadvantages, discussed in detail in a later section.

One important tactic if you are in contact with the media on a regular basis, or your company or organisation is frequently in the news, is to keep a log detailing your conversations and meetings with reporters. Enter the names of the journalist and publication, radio or television station; a contact number; the date of the contact; the reason for it; any information requested; any follow-up action needed; and, above all, how you responded. This log is useful for a number of reasons. It allows you to track media questions to identify particular interest in one area of your business: if so, you can then decide how best to take advantage of this. It permits you to look up previous answers so that you can be consistent in your responses. Furthermore, the entries should help settle any dispute over a journalist's accuracy, if you can prove that your reply was misquoted. Finally, the log will be invaluable if you are taken ill or on a day off when a story breaks, and someone has to step into your shoes at the last moment. Your painstaking record should at least give your colleague some of the answers.

Corrections

Journalists do, unfortunately, make mistakes from time to time. These errors may be insignificant and not worth worrying about, or they can be so serious they may have a devastating effect on your company. If a tabloid newspaper splashes across its front page that a food product your company makes is implicated in a cancer scare, but they have, in fact, confused your firm with another, then you clearly have very serious grounds for complaint. Your trade may well have suffered significantly and, apart from an apology and retraction from the paper, you may well have strong grounds for legal action.

It is also vital during an interview that if you think a journalist has misunderstood you, or may have taken some facts wrongly, you must correct these false impressions immediately. If you don't, you have only yourself to blame when a factually incorrect story appears. But don't lodge trivial complaints: if you spot an error - a misplaced initial, a slightly wrong specification, a misspelled name - weigh up carefully whether it is really worth the trouble of a formal complaint. A rebuke concerning a minor inaccuracy might ruin your relationship with a valued and trusted reporter.

Try to work out another way of amending the inaccuracy so that it does not appear to be an obvious correction. Journalists never like admitting to mistakes, and newspapers would prefer not to carry apologies or corrections if they can avoid it. But if you feel particularly aggrieved, and certainly if the error is a serious one, it is always worth contacting the journalist concerned and discussing things sensibly. A quiet chat may be all that is needed to get things put right.

Never overreact: it is especially pointless to lose your temper or threaten to go straight to the Editor. You should insist that a really bad mistake is corrected, though you may be able to agree a form of words which puts the reporter in a more favourable light. It may, for instance, be possible to correct the error simply by writing a new story which puts the record straight. That way, you get your correction and a second bite at the cherry, and avoid embarrassing the journalist.

But in situations where serious errors have been published, you can insist on a retraction of equal prominence: whether you get it will largely depend on your perseverance and determination. Alternatively, you could be offered the chance to state your views publicly in a "Letter to the Editor".

Serious errors should never go unchallenged, because there is always the risk that, if they are repeated, people will start to assume they must be true. So try to get a correction by appealing first to the journalist responsible and, if that fails, to the editor. If you still fail to get satisfaction, ask for the newspaper's appointed "complaints ombudsman" to investigate. Most newspapers, radio and television stations now have senior members of staff designated to handle complaints from readers, listeners and viewers, and an approach to them is usually enough to get redress.

One or two papers have appointed respected individuals outside the industry to act as the publication's ombudsman. A find in your favour could result in an official correction together with an apology for a serious error or, possibly, the chance to have the error corrected in another news story. In some circumstances the paper may even let you write the news story yourself. However, if the newspaper's ombudsman does not think you have been wronged, and provided you can establish that you or your organisation have been directly affected by the article, the way is open to you to take the matter to the Press Complaints Commission.

The **PRESS COMPLAINTS COMMISSION (PCC) as-sumed the duties of its predecessor, the Press Council, in 1991, operating from the same offices (No. 1, Salisbury Court, London EC4Y 8AE). The Commission has 15 mem-bers - seven editors, two former editors and six others -plus the chairman. The Commission came into being as a recom-mendation of the Calcutt Committee, reflecting growing concern about press behaviour in the areas of invasion of privacy and alleged sensationalism. In the opinion of many people, there has been some improvement in press stand-ards since the Commission - a more powerful body than the Council - began to function in earnest; there is, for instance, an agreed Code of Conduct for guidance to newspapers and stricter requirements for the acknowledgment of errors. The Code is available to the public, and can thus be cited in a complaint; its provisions are, in any case, always taken into consideration when the Council deals with a complaint.**

This is the procedure in the event of a genuine grievance (libel, defamation or simple unfair treatment by a newspa-per):

- **Try to resolve it with the publication as a preferred first step**

- If this approach fails, send the complaint, plus the offending article, to the PCC.
- As mentioned above, the complaint has to concern you or your organisation: you cannot complain on behalf of a third party.
- The PCC will refer the complaint to the newspaper Editor
- You may then receive a reply from the Editor, and see a printed retraction in the paper.
- However, if the Editor's response does not satisfy you, ask the PCC to give the complaint further consideration.
- The Commission's Director will draft an adjudication and circulate it among PCC members.
- If they approve it, the adjudication will be forwarded to the Editor for publication.
- If the Commission members disagree with the adjudication, it will be debated at their monthly meeting, and a final adjudication will then be made.
- The Editor may publish the full adjudication or a summary of it. This is not mandatory, but the practice is widely observed, even by the tabloid press.
- In fact, the PCC is on record as preferring stricter observance of its Code of Conduct to censure and method of publication.

The CODE OF CONDUCT is indeed the key document for complainants, who should cite in the complaint those sections alleged to have been breached. These are:

- Accuracy: This is a basic requirement of the Code. Errors and misleading material must be corrected promptly and "with due prominence", plus an apology where appropriate.
- Right of Reply: Publications are required to offer a "fair opportunity" for right of reply.
- Subterfuge: Ideally, journalists are not allowed to obtain information through misrepresentation, or to secure documents/photographs from people without their consent.

- Public Interest: This is the really delicate area, because those requirements listed as "subterfuge" can be breached where, in the opinion of the newspaper, it is "in the public interest" to do so. Areas of legitimate public interest include:
  - detecting or exposing crime/wrongdoing
  - exposing "antisocial conduct"
  - protecting public health/safety
  - correcting information/statements known to be deliberately misleading.

HARASSMENT:

Identifying harassment precisely is difficult enough; preventing it by legal means is probably impossible. It is an accusation which is easy to make and intractable to prove - and it can in any case be "justified" in the public interest. Harassment in popular (and PCC) terms certainly includes refusing to leave property when requested; photographing people on private property against their wishes and without permission; and telephoning them constantly. These matters might be resolved by a "Right to Privacy" Bill, but if that happened one certain result would be that a great many "guilty" people would escape the exposure they richly deserved.

FINANCIAL JOURNALISM: There are special considerations here. Journalists must not profit personally from advance, confidential information, nor pass information to others except on publication. They ought not to "puff" stock/shares in which they, or close members of their families, have an interest. They should not trade in shares they have tipped - or, more crucially, plan to tip.

CONFIDENTIALITY: Another ticklish subject. Journalists undoubtedly must honour their obligation to protect sources, but there are so many grey areas, and pitfalls not least for the journalists. Many have been heavily fined, or served jail sentences, for protecting sources needed to resolve legal actions.

THE BROADCASTING COMPLAINTS COMMISSION.

Should your complaint be against a radio or television programme or bulletin, follow the same procedure: ie, first try to contact the journalist responsible - or, failing that, his superior, normally the News Editor or Intake Editor, or the editor/producer of the offending programme.

You may well be surprised how quickly a major error will be corrected by a programme - though this does not necessarily apply to a news bulletin, which will simply put out a correct (but not obviously "corrected") version of the story in its next bulletin/summary.

Only as a second step should you complain directly to the Controller/Managing Director of the radio or television outlet involved. Going, as a first move, above the heads of both the reporter and his department will cause bitter and lasting resentment.

If both these approaches fail, the electronic media equivalent to the *Press Complaints Commission is the Broadcasting Complaints Commission (BCC) (Grosvenor Gardens House, 35-37 Grosvenor Gardens, London SW1W 0BS).*

The Commission was set up to consider complaints of unjust or unfair treatment in television, cable and radio programmes/outlets, and of unwarranted infringement of privacy; the Commission's remit includes associated advertising and teletext services.

The same considerations apply as with complaints to the PCC:
- Only a participant in a programme, or someone directly affected by the broadcast, can make a complaint. "Someone directly affected" clearly includes companies, or even companies as representative of their industries.

- The complaint will be ruled invalid unless you have first of all approached the requisite broadcasting authority and laid it before them.
- A complaint to the BCC - precisely detailed - has to be made in writing, and will include the title of the programme, and the date and channel on which it was broadcast.
- The complaint must fulfil these conditions to be found acceptable:
    - the allegations you are making must not concern a matter which is already the subject of legal proceedings in the United Kingdom
    - if there is an alternative remedy by way of legal proceedings, you must try that way first
    - the complaint must not be frivolous
    - it should be lodged with the Commission within a reasonable time of the broadcast.

- The Commission will copy the complaint to the relevant broadcasting authority, and request a programme transcript plus a written response. In the event that the authority has not actually made the programme - ie, it was produced by an independent programme maker - the complaint will be forwarded to the independent company.
- Complainants will be shown, and allowed to comment upon, the broadcaster's response. The broadcaster is then allowed the same freedom with your observations.
- Where the BCC differs from its print counterpart is that there is provision for a complainant to be invited to a private hearing of the matter, with the broadcaster present, to secure additional information from each side. In some instances, the two sides are seen separately.
- This process can last several weeks, but it must be completed before the Commission is able to reach a conclusion. The normal procedure then is for the BCC to instruct the broadcasting authority to publish the findings in the programme, and in either the Radio Times or TV Times (or other appropriate listings publication).

The BCC cannot compel broadcasters to apologise, or to broadcast a correction, or compensate for loss.

THE BROADCASTING STANDARDS AUTHORITY
This is a separate body, set up to handle complaints regarding the portrayal of violence and sex (and other matters of taste and decency) on radio and television, and in advertising and video films. The BSA is empowered to hold hearings, and to arrange for its findings to be published. The authority's address is 5-8 The Sanctuary, London SW1P 3JS.

Making Rich Lawyers Richer

If all attempts to seek redress for grossly distorted or prejudicial coverage fail, you have the final option of resorting to the courts, though this is an even slower (and hugely expensive) course to undertake. Bear in mind that the broadcasting organisations are very wealthy - and immensely experienced in the law of libel and defamation.

MEDIA TRAINING

Media training is crucial if your company or organisation enjoys a high profile, or could suddenly find itself in the media spotlight.

It is surprising how many senior management people in major companies have not had any training in dealing with the press, especially in how to cope when a radio or television reporter, brandishing a microphone, asks for an instant reaction to a big news story.

Some firms totally ignore the media and refuse all contact with it. This, of course, is a negative, even wasteful, attitude. The right editorial mention in the right journal can be worth far more than several pages of advertising.

It is obviously cheaper, has more credibility, and should be part of the corporate image-building process. Dealing successfully with the press is not merely a matter of answering a few questions, or issuing a press release.

Takeovers, especially hostile approaches, are a feature of industry today, and a well-produced media campaign is perhaps the most valuable weapon in fighting off an unwelcome assault.

THE CLEVEREST AND MOST PROSPEROUS FIRMS APPOINT:

- a senior manager to deal with the media
- skilled media trainers who can turn their executives into star performers
- an external media consultancy to hone their image - if they lack the in-house skills to do it themselves.

With that calibre of support, they should certainly be able to tackle anything the media is likely to throw at them. It is not, either, just large companies which can benefit from well-handled media relations.

Small businesses or purely local organisations or clubs can, with the co-operation of the local newspaper, run a campaign to recruit more members, raise more funds or simply enhance their business profile. They do this by scheduling a programme of events to generate a regular supply of news stories and photo opportunities.

There is no need to flood the paper with news, but if the organisation regularly appears in print once a month or thereabouts, potential sponsors will soon realise the advantages of becoming involved with them. And what works well for a mini-organisation will operate with equal success for a multi-national corporation - on a vastly greater scale, but with significant and comparable rewards.

Media training in all its facets is an integral tool in establishing business success and esteem. It teaches your executives not merely how to polish a performance on the electronic media, but how to use, to *manipulate*, the media to serve *your* interests.

It constitutes one of the wisest corporate investments your company or organisation could make, because it can help establish you at the forefront of your industry, and raise your profile to keep you in the position of market leader.

It is also a tax-efficient process: and that will please the shareholders, too.

The Journalist And His World

All newspapers have suffered as a result of recession and competition. All newspapers now have fewer journalists on staff than even two or three years ago, and most are reluctant to pay for outside contributions unless the story is really good. For the newspaper and the electronic journalist, the result has been a radical reappraisal of working techniques and lifestyles. Anyone who still believes that journalists spend their time drinking, enjoying free lunches and jetting off to exotic locations should spend a day with a national paper reporter.

On such a paper - and this applies to the big regional dailies as well - there are general reporters who work shifts and tackle any assignments the news desk throws at them. For stories already fitting into defined slots, the paper has specialist reporters and correspondents who cover particular areas: health, defence, crime, politics and so on.

The news desk is manned by the News Editor, who has overall control of the running of the news department. He or she will normally receive back-up from a number of assistant news editors to man the desk and oversee news-gathering. There is also a Diary Editor, responsible for allocating journalists to cover news assignments each day, and for keeping a detailed diary of forthcoming major news events. Working to the news room, but separate from it, are other news gathering departments specialising in court and parliamentary reporting, and covering sport and features.

Getting A Story In The Paper

Reporters write their copy and this is sent, now almost always by computer, to the subeditors' department. "Subs" are the people who knock news stories into shape on the screen. Some specialists handle only front-page stories, and others write just the headlines. A senior subeditor, known as a copy-taster, looks at all the stories coming in, and makes an editorial decision about which will be sent out and which will be "spiked" (ie, destined for the waste paper bin - albeit, these days, an electronic bin).

The copy-taster also decides the priority of each story, and roughly the length to which the finished version should run. The copy taster then assigns a subeditor to vet the copy, and correct or revise it as necessary. When the subeditor has finished, the story goes back to a revise-sub, whose job it is to look at the copy again to confirm that it is worthy of inclusion in the paper. If the story is accepted, it continues down the line and will ultimately finish up in the paper - though it may look nothing like it did when the reporter wrote it!

If a major news story breaks which will take up a lot of space, the revisesub has to decide which stories stay in the paper, and which are discarded. So a story written by a specialist reporter, subbed and accepted for publication, can still fall even at this late stage.

Out On The Job

Usually, a general reporter on a morning newspaper works to a shift pattern. The first day shift might start at around 10am, with journalists reporting to the news desk on arrival to pick up their assignments for the day. They may begin with a press conference and then go on elsewhere.

Press conferences almost always start late, so journalists have to wait around, wasting time, until the proceedings start. If a reporter has another job to cover, he or she may have only enough time to listen for a few minutes before leaving for the next assignment. In view of this, it is now a common practice - not just among the electronic media - to try to interview the principal speakers before the event starts. On their way out, reporters will want to pick up a press pack, which must give them all the information they would have got had they stayed for the whole press conference.

At some stage, of course, reporters have to return to base to write up their stories, or at least find a phone to put the copy over from a mobile computer. So unless journalists are assigned to a major news story which takes up all their working shift, an average day tends to pass in this manner: trailing from job to job around a crowded capital city, writing up as they go along, and filing as and when they can, covering probably three or four stories. And it can take 45 minutes to travel from one location to another.

41

Day In The Life Of A Specialist

Specialist reporters or correspondents usually have more control over their own diary and can decide which jobs are worth covering. But like general reporters, they will observe at all times one vitally important golden rule of journalism: keep in touch. From every new location, whether on a public phone or their own cellular phones, they will check in with the news desk, both to keep up-to-date with the story they are doing, and to relocate if another, more important, story breaks out.

The specialist's day normally starts with going through the mail and attending the first news desk editorial conference (the main conference, chaired by the Editor, takes place later). A specialist reporter on a national newspaper can receive a mini-mountain of mail every day.

On a reasonably busy day, a national paper or agency correspondent will get around 100 press releases, letters, faxes and reports. They receive only a cursory glance, but a snap judgement has to be made on each item. If a release looks interesting, it is put on one side; if it does not, it goes straight into the waste paper bin. Releases that are newsy and well-written receive immediate attention, and one or two of these are likely to be chosen as the basis for one of the stories in that day's output.

For the agency specialist, the aim would be to get one or two pieces on the wire as quickly as possible, so that late editions of the evening papers and early editions of the following day's morning papers would have copy coming in to handle - and radio and television news bulletins also had usable material. After the initial trawl through the mail and press releases, the specialist will make routine calls to Whitehall departments and other contacts, and return calls made to him. Then it is time to cover press conferences, briefings or other media events on the diary.

The specialist may have to sit through a two-hour lunch just to listen to a ten-minute speech by a Government Minister or industrialist. If you are required to do that on three or four days of the week, the very prospect of a slap-up lunch quickly loses its appeal. And with the need to stay sober for detailed note-taking and filing the story, whatever glamour remains quickly evaporates.

Then it is back to the office, or to Whitehall for an off-the-record briefing. A Government department may be publishing a White Paper or consultative document, in which case you have to attend an "officials only" briefing session, and rapidly scan the 300-page report to absorb the main points. Afterwards, you contact the relevant organisations for comments and reactions and finally get round to writing up your story.

It is not exactly cheering news to realise that all the other correspondents on your paper, agency or broadcasting outlet are busy doing exactly the same thing in *their* speciality areas - and that you are all are competing for a limited amount of space. If their stories turn out better than yours, you will have wasted an entire day, and possibly done irreparable damage to your already fragile digestive system.

Most specialists put in long hours, especially on a big story. Their leisure time, therefore, is jealously guarded, and calls to their homes should only be made if you really do have something important to say. **But remember:** if you have a really good and exclusive story, your contact will not mind what time of the night you phone him. Also, if an approach to you by a special contact does not result in the anticipated news story, it isn't only you who feels disappointment: the reporter himself will also be intensely frustrated.

The Television And Radio Reporter

A television reporter's day is often more action-packed, because television relies on pictures from the scene, whether it is a press conference or an air crash. Television news bulletins involve the newscaster, the occasional studio interview, frequent use of library "stock" film and graphics, and lots of action footage. To capture this last ingredient, a camera crew and journalist must travel to a scene, set up, record the item (or broadcast it "live" or by satellite link) and return to base to work on their story or move on to another assignment.

Compared with only a few years ago, most television organisations have reduced the number of camera crews on duty at any one time to save costs; a great deal of planning is therefore required to make sure that all major events are adequately covered.

The television reporter will not only research the story, but also fix the interviews and follow-up material, and write a script to lay on the film, plus cue material for the newscaster. On regional television programmes a reporter may well have several such interviews to do, either in the studio or on location, every day.

Radio reporters and correspondents lead equally hectic lives, with commitments to current affairs programmes (or a rolling news service) as well as to fixed point news bulletins and frequent news summaries. They will have to supply the programmes with feature packages, which involves editing a number of tapes, writing a script and running order for the inserts, and putting the whole thing together with a producer in the studio.

And, of course, each item on the news bulletin or in the body of a programme, must run to a stated and precise time. If a late recorded piece overruns, it could throw the timing out for an entire bulletin, which could lead to the reporter doing his piece "live", and trimming it on air as he goes along. Bulletin and programme editors tend to go a funny colour when this happens.

Whether at home or abroad, journalists can face appalling dangers. A "home" story like Northern Ireland has produced a crop of injuries and anxiety neurotics, and abroad, where the greater danger tends to be, the number who have lost their lives covering situations like Bosnia and Somalia bears tragic testimony to the peril in which journalists are regularly placed in trying to do their jobs. It is, of course, simply part of that job: nothing more, nothing less.

Chapter 3

PRESS RELEASES

Every day, thousands of people from press offices, public relations companies, Government departments, local authorities, business and industry, clubs and societies and a host of other sources, sit down to write press releases for use in the media. Every day, *almost* everything these people turn out is thrown away unused. This chapter deals with writing a press release to capture the attention of the reader. There are also reproductions of a selection of press releases, good and bad, actual and fictitious, with analyses and expert advice.

The Nature Of A Press Release

Although there is now less space for news in most newspapers, due to a reduced number of pages, that is not the reason why the vast majority of press releases don't make it into print. They are discarded because, for the most part, they are appallingly bad.

The press release can be a very useful weapon in the publicist's arsenal. The format allows a company or public relations consultant to send out the same story to as many newspapers, magazines, radio and television outlets as they choose. If they get the mailing right, their press releases should arrive at the right time to secure massive publicity - provided they are good enough.

Sophisticated press releases can be tailored to suit the particular media sectors at which they are aimed: the requirements of a national newspaper are different from those of a local weekly, and a trade magazine also has its own special needs. But the main requirement of all the media is a press release which provides a good story, contains all the relevant information, is topical (ie, it didn't happen two weeks ago) and, above all, can be used with the minimum of fuss.

Unfortunately, what most papers actually get is something far removed from that ideal. It is commonplace to receive a news release with no date - or a date so old as to make it a document of almost historic interest. If the release is undated, but the story looks interesting, the journalist has to go to the trouble of ringing someone up to find out when the release was written, and when the events described in it took place.

That may sound simple enough, but assuming there is a telephone number for further information - and it is alarming how often this is missing - there is no guarantee they will be immediately available. With a deadline approaching, a journalist who cannot get an answer for perhaps several hours is more than likely to drop the story and pass on to something more rewarding.

Press releases can and do work when all the ingredients are right. If you want to reach a wide audience, a press release is one answer, provided you can negotiate the minefield that has to be crossed in writing and sending it out. The successful press release will have three essential elements:

- it must tell a good story
- the timing has to be right
- it must be correctly targeted.

It sounds deceptively easy, but since the vast majority of press releases written by professional public relations consultants go straight into the bin, there are clearly problems which have not been overcome.

It has been calculated that discarded press releases cost those public relations companies, and ultimately the firms for whom they are acting, about £70m a year. Apart from the horrendous waste of time, such exercises seriously damage the credibility of the public relations firm and the company it is representing. Journalists are quick to recognise the company name, or that of the public relations firm handling them, and this causes warning bells to ring. A succession of ineffectual news releases can lead to a journalist automatically undervaluing, or even dismissing on sight, everything else coming from that source. This kind of damage takes an enormous effort to repair.

However, the advantages that can be gained by getting things right are as great as, if not greater than, the disadvantages when it goes wrong. Journalists are quick to spot the news potential of a well-presented press release, and if it is written in a style that can be easily adapted for that particular paper, it is even more welcome. The journalist will take credit for the story, but that is of small consequence so long as it is used. The aim, after all, is simply to get it into print.

The other advantage of a press release over an interview or tip-off is that you have the opportunity to put down on paper exactly what you want to convey. You can also control the facts and quotes, and the release timing.

Bear in mind that a specialist journalist may get up to 400 press releases and reports in his mail each week. He can afford to spare only a few seconds to absorb each press release, and in that time he must be able to assess the value of the story it is trying to tell. What he hopes to find is:

- a story/news angle which can be immediately developed
- or at least material of potential interest as a story or feature
- material that can be easily assimilated
- a release that contains all the relevant facts
- a set of good quotes
- a contact number for follow-ups, quotes or pictures.

That is what the journalist *wants*, but not normally what he *gets*. The sad fact is that most press releases are turgid and badly written. They may contain glaring contradictions; but whatever else they are, they are not news.

A press release simply announcing the launch of a new electrical product may be suitable for a trade journal specialising in that area, but it is not going to be used by a national newspaper - so sending it to one is both naive and inept targeting. Yet if the electrical product is the first of its type, capable of doing spectacular things, costs a fortune or is incredibly cheap, or has anything else about that is unusual, that release could be written to attract the interest of the nationals.

Press releases about the "world's first", "Britain's biggest" and so on, stand a better than average chance of being used. Most press releases fail because they omit even the most basic details. A release on a controversial subject that leaves out a contact number, so that its authenticity can be checked and the story followed up, is almost certain to die a swift death.

It is not difficult to construct a press release which is as near perfect as possible. Provided the story is authentic and newsworthy, the release must fulfil the requirements outlined above, and also observe conventions like listing Christian names rather than initials, and omitting technical jargon and unfamiliar abbreviations.

On these last points, it is infuriating for the journalist to spend valuable time trying to find out whether Mr F Smith is Frank or Frederick, as both are listed as company directors.

Preparing The Press Release

If you have something worth saying to the media in a press release, you must get it right the first time. You cannot send out a press release which contains only half the story because it will not be used, but it will damage your credibility as a reliable source of information. Equally, unless you are adroit, you will not be able to retry a press release that fails to make it the first time round. Some media experts are capable of redrafting and re-angling a press release for a second shot, but not if it is tied to a particular event and date. Redrafting is a skilled job: think it through carefully before deciding to give a story a completely fresh angle.

BASIC RULES

The ground rules are simple:

- keep it factual, accurate and to the point
- use a headline that tells the story
- date the release
- put all the main points in the first paragraph
- include quotes/comments from a named spokesperson, giving first name and correct title
- avoid jargon
- list a contact name and office/home phone numbers.

All these categories are essential practice:

Headlines

The headline conveys an instant understanding of what the story is about. It should encapsulate the theme in a single line, but there is a case to be made for writing a headline so intriguing that the journalist feels compelled to read on. The headline you write is unlikely ever to appear in print: that is the task of a subeditor, who is immensely skilled at it, especially on the tabloid newspapers. Another reason for not using your headline is that one of the competitor newspapers might, in spite of everything, decide to, so generally speaking no-one does. A snappy headline is wasted unless it is backed up by the press release. One (among many) releases which committed this cardinal sin came from an estate agent with branches throughout the country, and a large press and public relations department. The release was sent to property correspondents on national and major regional morning newspapers. The headline read: "Country home sold for record price"; this would certainly have been enough to persuade property correspondents to read on.

The problem was that the release did not mention the record price at all. To add insult to injury, the last paragraph read: "The sale, to a private party, was for an undisclosed amount". The estate agent's press office finished with egg on their face, reluctantly admitting that they were unable to disclose the sale price - because it had been agreed not to make it public! Needless to say, the press release did not get any publicity.

Date

A date on the press release tells the journalist it is topical. A press release sent out some time before you actually want it to appear should state the date of publication clearly. If it is an important story, and damage might be caused by premature publication, you can put an embargo on it. Broadly speaking, though, embargoes should be used only when absolutely essential.

Don't bother to distribute a press release about something which happened days/weeks ago unless there is a good reason. A three-week-old jumble sale raising £120 might be worth a paragraph, but it is much better to find a new angle - how the money, for example, has been, or will be, spent. It is more impressive to be able to say that: "Twenty lucky children will enjoy a free day at the seaside thanks to the fund-raising efforts of....", rather than: "A jumble sale held to raise funds for the local Round Table raised £120....."

There are occasionally times when an old story can still be news. One instance would be newspaper coverage, going back months, of a long-distance walker's bid to be the first to cross the Himalayas; clearly, it could be several days before the news comes through that the walk has been successfully completed. In that event the fact that the story is old doesn't matter. The crossing is still news, because it hasn't been reported before.

First Paragraph

Getting this right is vital: the first paragraph might be all the journalist has time to read, so the release must be riveting enough to command immediate attention.

Hype And Plug

Avoid hype at all costs. You have to sell your story, and that may mean using adjectives like "biggest", "best", "first" and so on, but don't overdo it. You can get carried away by hyperbole, and when a reporter checks the release he may find that things are not quite as you have portrayed them. Similarly, if a journalist suspects you have exaggerated one aspect of the story, he will treat the rest with suspicion and may decide it is safer not to use it at all. Leave the hype to the newspapers: they are actually good at it.

Plugs (for your company/organisation) can also be grossly overdone. A press releases that begins with a company name and goes on to mention it three times in every subsequent paragraph is too blatant. There are more subtle ways of putting a message, and name, across. One is simply to devise an original and upbeat quote, which you can then attribute to the managing director of the client company - using his full name and title. The quote will undoubtedly add to the story, so it will be sourced - and there is the plug, achieved by stealth, without undue emphasis.

Yet every day, too many press releases of the wrong type - they start with a company name, they are over-hyped and flagrantly plugged - arrive in newspaper offices all over the country. One reason is that releases are often properly written by skilled public relations people, only to be altered by the client company when they are sent for approval. Apart from the city pages, look through your national newspaper and see how many stories actually do start with the name of a company. Articles might frequently open with the name of a person, but rarely with that of a company, arguably because if smacks too glaringly of advertising. There is nothing wrong with mentioning the company name later on in the first paragraph - in fact, you should take care to do so.

Style tips: Avoid archaic and unnecessary words. "While" is better than "whilst", "about" is preferable to, and shorter than, "approximately"; and why use terms like "establish", "utilize" and "manufacture" when "set up", "use" and "make" are available. Single-figure numbers are normally spelled out, but use actual figures for 10 and upwards.

Make an exception for prices: £2m is better than "two million pounds". And use "more than £2m" rather than "over £2m". With numbers or amounts, a smaller quantity is always "fewer than" as opposed to "less than" in front of the number. Write out "per cent" rather than use the "%" abbreviation and, in English language publications, use "am" and "pm" for times rather than the 24-hour clock.

There are many rules of style; they can vary from newspaper to newspaper and the best outlets tend to have their own Style Books. So read the newspapers for style as well as content, and use that knowledge when targeting press releases.

A press release must encompass as succinctly as possible everything you have to say: apart from that, there is no cast-iron rule about how long it should be. Most releases run to one or two pages, and there is rarely room in a newspaper for a release longer than this. You could run to three or more pages for a particularly complicated story, but unless it is intended for use as a feature, it will have to be reduced in size considerably by the subeditor, and material you wanted mentioning could be cut out.

For a pointed summing-up of press release style, follow the advice of a Fleet Street news editor:
- keep it simple and interesting
- avoid flowery and technical language
- imagine you are telling a story to a friend, then write it down in the same relaxed manner
- don't try to be literary
- concentrate on the facts
- ask yourself
    WHAT is the event about?
    WHY is it being held?
    WHEN is it taking place?
    HOW is it being organised?
    WHERE is it taking place?
    WHO is involved?
    HOW can they be contacted?

According to the news editor in question: "If you answer all these questions succinctly and clearly you should have a good press release".

Layout

How the press release is set out can be just as important as its content. A four page A4 document, closely typed on both sides of each page, is going to take a news editor or journalist a long time to read to decide whether there is a story. If the journalist is in a hurry, the chances are that the document will be put on one side to deal with something else which is more usable. So by the time further attention is paid to your lengthy press release it will be too late to use it, or something more important has cropped up which will get precedence. It could end up in the waste bin without ever having been properly read.

Ideally, press releases should be sent out on strongly designed, eye-catching press release stationery. This will clearly indicate the name of your company or organisation, and the address, telephone and fax numbers, and will have the words "Press Release" written in bold letters somewhere at the top of the page. Special press release stationery is important, because if you send out a lot of releases, journalists should soon be able to recognise yours fairly quickly, even if it is tucked into a sheaf of competitors.

Lay The Release Out Like This:

- at the top put your name, address and the organisation
- leave enough space between the letterhead and the start of the text for the subeditor's instructions
- type the release in double (or one and a half lines) spacing on one side of the paper only
- leave wide margins for subbing and corrections
- write short, pithy sentences of 25-30 words
- use no more than three sentences to a paragraph
- clearly indicate if the press release is going over on to a second page
- never split a paragraph between pages
- clearly number each page and write "End" at the bottom of the last page
- fasten the pages together with a paper clip so they don't get separated: *never* use a staple.

Don't underline words or use capitals to highlight things which you think are important: that is for the journalist to decide. **Remember:** contacts are the life-blood of any journalist, and most will copy new names and phone numbers into their contact book. If, for example, you represent a holiday company or a local charity, your name could be useful if a story breaks in the appropriate area, and the journalist needs to get hold of someone quickly for a reaction, comment or just a good quote.

Embargoes

The embargo system was created to help journalists prepare difficult stories in advance of publication. Because of parliamentary protocol, for instance, Government White Papers normally have to be presented first to the House of Commons, so publication is scheduled to coincide with when the House is sitting, and often when the Minister responsible for the report is answering questions.

However if, say, the Department of Health is issuing a major report running to several hundred pages at 3.30pm, it doesn't give journalists much time to read through the document and write their stories if the page on which the copy is to appear is printed at 6.30pm that evening. Correspondents/reporters covering the story not only have to write their pieces, they may have to interview the Minister responsible, speak to Departmental civil servants if extra facts or statistics are required, and perhaps to several other organisations affected by the report's recommendations. The story has then to be subbed and tailored to fit the space allocated for it in the paper.

Because the Government is just as anxious as any other organisation to get maximum publicity, it often allows journalists access to reports in advance, on the strict understanding that nothing will appear in print or be broadcast before the stipulated time. The embargo system is widely used: companies will often issue their annual reports in advance to selected, "trusted" journalists under the same arrangement.

Politicians are notoriously keen to distribute copies of their speeches in advance. A politician making a major after-dinner speech is not likely to stagger to his feet until 10.30pm, so a reporter will be unable to get copy into next morning's newspaper if he/she has to sit through the entire speech, and then phone the story back to the office. By that time, the first editions of the morning papers are already printed and being distributed. So by handing out copies of the speech in advance, but under embargo, politicians can normally expect their words to appear in print the following day.

Occasionally, accidents happen. A minister may distribute copies of a speech being made that night through his/her agent or press officer, and then be taken ill at the last minute. By the time word of the cancellation comes through, the speech might already have been written up - and the newspaper printed. It is not too uncommon, therefore, to read in the papers the words of a speech that was never delivered.

Another example: the Queen's New Year and Birthday Honours Lists are normally made available early, under strict embargo, for newspapers to prepare the several pages of copy they normally devote to them. Unfortunately, the embargo system is now widely abused. Certain newspapers and radio programmes quite flagrantly break embargoes in order to "scoop" (or "beat", as they prefer to say) their competitors. As a result, some Fleet Street (and other) papers are no longer given access to advance copies of embargoed documents, and the rest have been subject to tighter controls.

Perhaps the most glaring breach of an embargo in recent years has been the early publication of the Queen's traditional Christmas Day speech. The newspapers that broke the embargo did so because they hoped publication would boost sales or ratings -and, like it or not, that is the most important consideration as far as most news outlets are concerned.

Embargoes should be used only if they are absolutely necessary. In most cases they are not. Use one if you must, but be ready to act immediately if it is broken by just one newspaper. Should this happen, the other papers might ask you to lift the embargo - or they may just go ahead and publish anyway, since the news has already been made public.

Here is a typical embargo, displayed clearly in bold type at the top of the document:

EMBARGO: NOT FOR PUBLICATION, BROADCAST OR USE ON CLUB TAPES BEFORE 0001HRS MONDAY 5 MAY 1994.

This means that a morning newspaper can, of course, carry the story in its Monday morning edition, which will not usually be available until after the embargoed time. Radio and television can use the material for the first time in their midnight bulletins, provided it is *after* one minute past midnight.

Press Release Targeting

Targeting press releases to try to ensure they reach the right audience is crucial. Every magazine and newspaper has a theme, a style, a preferred length for news stories and features. Try to follow these. It is often better to write several press releases and target them to specific outlets than to send out a general release which may be of interest to very few.

It really isn't difficult to tailor-make press releases for various target audiences, and the effort is more than justified. In recent years, surveys have become a fashionable (and rewarding) method of getting publicity. Almost every day you can read in the papers about some survey or other, looking at our eating habits, our attitude to foreigners, how often we use deodorants, and so on. These surveys usually get coverage because first, we all like to know how we compare with other people generally, and whether we are "average" or exceptional; and secondly, we are even more interested to learn how we compare with our neighbours and friends.

A newsy survey containing regional comparisons can be tailored, localised and "personalised" in as many as a dozen or more individual press releases. For instance, the Yorkshire Post would get a story pointing out how Yorkshire people rate better than - or below - the national average, and then how they compare with people in other parts of the country. The press releases for the Scotsman, Newcastle Journal, Brighton Evening Argus and other important provincial papers will need only a little alteration to give them strong local and regional angles, which greatly increase the chances of publication.

People Targeting

Many people are under the mistaken impression that press releases addressed, say, to particular specialists actually reach them. This is not necessarily the case. Most mail going into a newspaper office is opened by an editorial assistant, who hands it to a News Editor or deputy news editor to look through. The News Editor decides which items should be followed up by his team of reporters, and the remainder of the post is delivered via the internal mail system to whoever seems the appropriate person to receive it, assuming there is no named addressee.

By this time, the envelopes have usually been thrown away, so although a specialist may have asked for vital information from a particular source, unless there is an accompanying letter to make this clear, the material could well end up going to someone else who, not knowing the relevance of it, will more often than not just throw it away.

Spruce Up Your Filing System

It is important to keep media files up-to-date, so that you know the names of the specialists you want to deal with. There are few things more annoying for a specialist than to receive a letter addressed to the person who occupied his/her chair many years before. If you are sending out an important release, a phone call alerting the journalist to it is also a good idea, because he or she will then look out for it, or prime the news desk, who will know where to direct it when it arrives. The phoned tip-off might also alert the journalist that a good news story is about to break; the relevant files can be summoned from the library to prepare background information.

Get The Timing Right

Timing is of paramount importance. The press release must arrive in good time, and it is surprising how many come in too late to be followed up, or too long after the event. For morning and evening papers, you should aim the press release to land at least 24 hours before you want it to appear in the paper.

Obviously, if a big story breaks and you have to send a press release out in a hurry, you will have to operate within the remaining time available. Always contact the paper and tell the news desk/correspondent that the release is on its way via fax or messenger.

For weekly and Sunday papers, you need to get your press release in several days before publication day. And lead-in times for many magazines mean that your release may have to be sent in a month, or even more, before the journal hits the news stands. Always make it absolutely clear when you want the release to be published. Print **FOR IMMEDIATE RELEASE** at the top of the first page if the story can be used straight away.

If you are sending it out several days in advance, make sure this is also clearly stated. You can place an embargo on the release if you think it is justified - but there are risks in this, as discussed earlier. The danger in sending a release out too early is that, even if it is a good story, it might get lost before the paper has had a chance to use it. Alternatively, if you were hoping the press release might generate publicity for a forthcoming show or charity match, and it is used too early, people may forget about it in the period between publication and the event taking place.

Timing is important for other reasons. You can take advantage of an up-coming major news story that could be reflected in an event with which you are concerned. By referring in your press release to the bigger news story, you are more likely to win a mention than if you had concentrated just on your own local event.

Again, if a report is due out which might criticise your organisation or industry, it is obviously good tactics to time a press release to arrive in the newspaper office as the journalist is writing his story on the report. By doing this, you may well induce the journalist to include your statement in the story, or the reporter could even ring you up if you are openly critical of the report. After all, "Government report slammed...." makes a better story than "The Government today published its long awaited guidelines on...."

This presupposes, of course, that you know what is in the report. Even if you do not know precisely what the document recommends, you should have a pretty good idea. There will probably have been leaks in the papers, and if the report concerns an area that affects you or your company, rumours would have been flying around for weeks. As a last resort, you or someone else from the company will have tried to get a "steer" from a member of the committee producing the report, or from somebody who gave evidence to it.

At any event, it is preferable to have a statement - issued through a press release - used at the same time as the story about publication of the report. Once that story has appeared, the newspapers will almost certainly lose interest. If a paper does carry your views after the report has been published then your statement will not achieve the same degree of prominence as the original story. There might even be the suggestion of "sour grapes" about an attack on a Government report some time after it has appeared. While this is probably unfair, people are only too ready to think: "Well they would say that, wouldn't they?".

Pre-Emptive Strike

Bear in mind that the "pre-emptive strike" press release is an effective, powerful and even dangerous weapon. Assume you have been told that a highly sensitive report is being published on, say, Wednesday of the following week, which is likely to be strongly critical of your company. One course open to you would be to send out a press release for publication on the Tuesday, casting doubt on the findings of the report due to be published the next day. What would your release contain? Well, you might, for example, have a perfectly legitimate story citing new scientific research which shows that the report is already out of date. By getting your story in first, you steal considerable thunder from the report's publication.

And if you cast enough doubt on the report's credibility, the national papers may decide not to publish it at all - or the Press Association even to send it out! You will then have won a commercially vital propaganda victory for your company or client.

In any case, you'll find that most news desks will tell you if an event you are planning is likely to clash with something else, or whether a major news event is taking place on the day you plan to issue a press release. For instance, there is not much point in putting out a press release on Budget Day unless you want to react to something the Chancellor has said. The following day's newspapers devote so much space to the Budget, and what it means, that most other news just gets squeezed out.

So pick the time carefully to aim for maximum exposure. There are good days and bad days, good times - and very bad times. One extremely good time is a quiet Saturday evening: the Press Association sends out a bundle of news stories on the wire at 9am every Sunday, so that early duty sub-editors on national and regional morning newspapers have lots of good copy for the inside pages of Monday's papers. A similar service goes out at 4.30am each weekday morning to provide early copy for evening papers up and down the country. These stories get a lot of exposure because they reach the newspaper offices at exactly the time they are needed.

Check to see what else is happening before mailing a press release. Avoid coinciding with a larger event which will possibly dominate the news pages, but try to tie-in with it, or at least to associate with anything else happening which could boost the chances of your press release being used. Get the timing right, and you increase the likelihood of your press release being used - and that is what it is all about.

Distribution

Remember to keep a log of media contacts, especially in a crisis. In fact the log should be an integral part of a wider directory of the journalists whom you regularly meet or even talk to. Ensure that it is periodically updated. Learn the value of maintaining media lists, ideally on a computer, so that you can revise easily, and print out addresses quickly.

These lists can be broken down into groups:
- National morning papers
- National Sunday papers
- National radio and television outlets
- Regional morning papers
- Regional evening papers
- Regional Sunday papers
- Regional radio and television
- Local radio
- Major weekly groups
- Individual weeklies and freesheets
- General consumer magazines
- Specialist consumer magazines
- Trade magazines

You won't need an actual dossier on each candidate, but the list should contain contact names, addresses (office and home), telephone and fax numbers (office and home). Organise the contacts into specialist areas so that you can pull up lists for city editors, show business/agriculture/industrial correspondents, news editors, picture editors, and so on, whatever suits your industry or client best, depending on requirements.

The advantage of having this information on file is that if you suddenly find yourself in the middle of a crisis, and have to distribute a press release in a hurry, at least the mail-out will be the easiest part. For source material, you can get the addresses and telephone numbers of local and regional newspapers, and local and regional radio and television from the telephone directory. Ring up the paper, radio or television station and ask for the names of the news editor, specialist reporter or picture editor and check on telephone numbers for direct desk lines to enable you to bypass the switchboard.

Find out if there is more than one fax number you can use. Faxing an urgent press release can be frustrating if the number is engaged, so it helps to have a back-up number which ordinary members of the public may not know. For more detailed lists of newspaper, radio and television station addresses, you can either buy or subscribe to specialist directories if you are likely to use them repeatedly, or you should be able to get the information from the local library, which ought to stock copies of media directories. The main ones in the field are Benn's, the Blue Book of Broadcasting, PIMS and Two Ten. These directories are regularly updated and give you not only details about all newspapers - from nationals to weeklies - and magazines, but also all the specialist writers.

58

The Follow-Up

Finally, try your hardest to find a follow-up angle to the press release so that if the story does really well, and attracts a lot of attention, you can get a second bite at it. For example, if you issue a release about a new product, the follow-up could be a big improvement in export orders, or how the factory is working flat out to cope with demand, or how extra staff have had to be taken on. A story promoting a food safety campaign could be followed by a release saying how successful it has been, and how plans are already under way to repeat the exercise next year.

Summary

To summarise, a press release must tell a story, it must be well-written, relevant, clear, succinct - and complete. It should not be an obvious plug, although one of the skills in writing it is to get away with the not so obvious plug.

It must not be too long, nor mislead, nor appear to be little more than advertising. You have to send it to the right person at the most opportune time. And, above all, it must be better than all the others flooding into the newspaper on that particular day!

Photo Opportunities

It is often said that a good picture is worth a thousand words. It may sound cliched, but it is true. Always look for good photo opportunities, which can be utilised in one of two ways. There is the "photo call", in which you invite press photographers, and television if the story is strong enough, to come in and photograph the event you are organising; and there is the "photo story", where you submit photographs and copy to the papers in the hope that they will be published.

Try to exercise as much control as possible about the timing of the event. There is no point in staging it late in the afternoon if you are hoping to get television coverage in the early evening news bulletin. Equally, unless absolutely unavoidable, don't organise events for Saturday afternoons, when most press photographers will be assigned to covering sports fixtures.

Try to give Picture Editors as much notice as possible about the time and date, and subject matter. Never assume that a news desk will automatically pass on to the picture desk information about photo opportunities. Odd as it may seem, communication between newspaper departments is often appalling.

Conference Time

Most newspapers hold weekly and daily editorial conferences. At the weekly get-together of departments, all forthcoming events over the coming week are discussed, and decisions taken about which will be covered and in what detail - and which will not be covered, either because they are not considered newsy enough, or simply because there is not enough manpower available. Each day, there is a similar conference to look at that day's news stories and, possibly, the major events on the following day. At either of these conferences, the News Editor might start talking about an event coming up which the picture desk knows nothing about, and vice versa.

However, if an event is in the news picture diary in good time, the Picture Editor can plan ahead and even call in an extra photographer if necessary, or commission a freelance photographer to cover for the paper. Nearer the actual date, send in final details of the event with times, dates, locations and contact names and numbers. It is also good practice to ring the picture desks a few days beforehand to check if they have the event on their diary, and if they plan to cover it.

Most Picture Editors will be non-committal, unless it is a very good story. They are rarely able to guarantee a photographer's attendance, because they never know what major news stories may break and clash with it. And, like press conferences, never assume that because three press photographers are scheduled to attend, they will all actually turn up. They may well be on their way to cover your event when they get a call from their picture desk diverting them to cover something else.

It is therefore important to have your own photographer available - one who can quickly produce prints for media distribution.

If your organisation does not run to an in-house photographer and there is no amateur on the staff who can take photographs of a high enough quality, then you must hire one for the occasion. The advantage of getting in professionals is that they will be able to process the film immediately after the event, so you can make your selections of the best photographs and distribute them. It is always a good idea to ring the local paper (even if it is not a purely local story) for advice. The Picture Editor will be able to give you the names of reliable freelances, or local specialist photographers whom the paper itself uses from time to time. These photographers know the kind of picture the newspaper prefers, and they will already have a relationship of trust with the paper.

Sometimes, a local paper photographer who is off duty can be persuaded to take the photographs, and again this gives you an edge.

"D-Day"

The photographer must be fully briefed about your requirements, and you will obviously be at the event yourself to supervise matters and to ensure you get what you want. If something unexpected occurs, you are able to make on-the-spot decisions which others may not be prepared to do. The briefing to the photographer should be specific: tell him/her the pictures you want, and why you want them. (For instance, at an event organised to welcome a fund-raising celebrity, you do not want to see the photographer snapping away at everyone but the celebrity).

The photographer will also need to know whether to supply black and white prints, colour transparencies, or both; and don't forget to pass on special requests from newspapers or magazines - and check the orders are filled. One trade magazine may have asked for a particular shot: it is worth going to the trouble of taking it, because it will mean extra publicity in a specialist magazine which everyone working in your industry is likely to read.

While the event is in progress, let the professional get on with his work. Don't fuss, or dance around looking agitated: you will probably get in the frame and spoil a picture or two. And be flexible with your requirements: unexpected photo opportunities do present themselves; either you or the photographer ought to spot them and take advantage of them. You will find that the professional photographer will always take many more pictures than you could conceivably need. But don't stop him: he knows what he is doing.

He will probably produce a contact-print sheet for you to make a final choice of pictures. In any case, it is always worth having more prints than you require for immediate distribution, since they will be useful when you get round to putting together the staff magazine, or the company's annual report. And you never know when the Chairman's wife will ring you insisting on an immediate print of a particular shot for her family album.

Pictures Tell Stories

Almost any situation or event can lend itself to a photograph but, as with press releases, far more pictures get thrown into a newspaper's waste bin than ever make it on to the news pages. That is why, if you decide to take your own photographs and circulate them to the media, you have to come up with something different or at least persuasive. A head-and-shoulders photograph of a building society's new area manager might find a home in the local paper, but it is hardly an inspiring picture.

A much better shot would be of the manager arriving at the office, and all the staff lined up outside to greet him/her. In this way, there are more people in the frame, the name of the building society will appear in the photograph as well as in the caption (make sure the name is clearly visible in the background!), and you have added interest value to an everyday situation, which will please the newspaper. People who use the building society, and friends and relatives of the staff, will recognise their faces in the paper, and order extra copies. Even disinterested outsiders will be encouraged to study that sort of picture more closely than they would the straightforward head-and-shoulders, just to find out what is going on.

So there is no inducement to stick to traditional ideas and practices about taking photographs. Prizewinners at a talent show need not be lined up like a "firing-squad": inject elements of action and interest in every picture you commission. Devise interesting compositions to tell the story, or spell out a message. Provided it has a strong news interest, a picture taken on the factory floor showing a number of people working together with smiles on their faces, also suggests a happy environment. Arrange for it to display the "corporate" branding as well - but not too blatantly!

People add interest to a picture, as well as selling papers. A photograph of a new office block, showing the building alone, is boring. It's much better to line up the staff in tiers in front of the building, or standing around while the managing director cuts a tape on the front door: and better still to involve celebrities, or local personalities such as the Mayor or Member of Parliament, because this will increase the chance of the photograph being used.

Another example: a photograph of a new headmaster sitting behind a desk is not likely to attract more than passing attention, but if the head is pictured addressing his first school assembly, or meeting his staff, it gives the setting an element of action that was missing, and also indicates the scope of his duties by showing how many pupils and staff he is responsible for. It is a plus factor newswise - and visually more compelling - to show people in their working environment and in the context of their responsibilities.

A photograph of four men standing in a row showing off the long-service awards they have just received tells you nothing about the sort of people they are - or even what they do, beyond the bare departmental description. A more interesting and informative picture could have been taken of the same group of men at their place of work, where you can see them doing the job which they have done (with historical variations, which the caption would explain) for 40 years!

Make The Right Choice

Deadlines will often make the production of contact sheets ("mini"-photographs of all the shots taken) impossible but, if there is time to spare, they are handy for choosing the best ones to use for your mail-out. Newspaper technology is now so advanced that papers can take black and white photographs from colour prints and transparencies, and may even use colour, but most still prefer good glossy black and white photographs enlarged to 10" x 8". You must check whether the paper uses colour, and if they prefer prints or transparencies. Clearly, the photographer needs to know this in advance so that he has the right film in the camera! Once you have made your selection, the photographer can enlarge the required number of prints.

Words

Whatever the subject matter of the photograph, it must be accompanied by either a caption or an expanded story. The caption allows you to give brief details which are not obvious from the photograph itself.

A picture of four men, one holding a large trophy, sitting on the back of a milk float in front of the local dairy, indicates that a group of men associated with the dairy in some way have won a cup. Theoretically, all the caption needs to do is explain who the men are, what they have won, when and where. Try to add an extra level of news interest which the four men could provide from their own backgrounds (ie, one might have worked for the dairy all his life; another could be a keen gardener, a union official, or a special constable). Learn more about the men than their names and you will greatly improve an otherwise static photograph.

Treat the caption as you would a longer and more important news story. It is imperative that it should be worded correctly and contain all the necessary information, and that it is attached in the approved way to the picture. Even though it is only a caption, it must always carry a contact name and telephone number.

NEVER write on the back of a photograph, because you are likely to leave an impression on the front which may render it useless. Type the caption on a piece of paper and then sellotape this to the back of the photograph. The caption will stay in position as the print is handled in the picture news room, and can be safely removed when the picture goes down to processing.

Finally, you may consider that the photograph, with even a deep caption, cannot tell the whole story; you will then need to send out more details in the form of a press release, which should follow the guidelines set out earlier.

Distribution

If you are working to tight deadlines, photographs should be hand or courier-delivered, otherwise they can go in the post. **But mail the photographs in special hard-backed envelopes which will protect them.**

****

SAMPLE PRESS RELEASES

First a pair of instructive examples from a top-flight media and public relations consultant. These are not actual press releases, but examples used by the agency itself to illustrate good and bad practice. Also reproduced are their analyses and expert advice.

MAJOR CONTRACT FOR LEADING CARRIER

Britain's number one carrier, Royal Mail Parcels, has landed a MAJOR NEW contract with ABC Ltd - the country's biggest supplier of electronic components.

Marketing Director, Peter Child, acclaimed the ABC contract as a great achievement, saying it "is one of the most sought-after contracts in the whole of the distribution business.

"ABC has gone for us because they realised that no-one else could match the Post Office for its professionalism, its network or our range of highly developed services".

ABC will be using Datapost, Super 24, Super 48 and Standard service to send its products speedily on their way to their nationwide destinations.

Royal Mail Parcels unrivalled distribution network will be running at peak performance to guarantee success for ABC. Its unmatched delivery fleet, which carries over 250 million items a year, will be used to reach ABC's huge network of 2000 outlets.

"We chose Royal Mail Parcels because they proved to us that they had the products, the pedigree and the reliability to match our needs", commented ABC's General Manager, John Smith.

With ABC's distribution needs extending across the whole of the country, RMP has proved yet again that it is the only carrier that can really deliver the goods to meet such a major distribution challenge.

As Peter Brown, District Manager of the RMP distribution centre pointed out: "We will be using all the services at our disposal to make sure that ABC is a satisfied customer. These services range from express services such as

Datapost and Super 24 to our guaranteed 5-day standard delivery service. ABC has bought the best by buying RMP".

The unique combination of services available to ABC Ltd shows, said Peter Child, that "RMP is truly the best choice for business customers".

That is the release as set out by the agency on genuine RMP press release paper. Here is the agency's verdict on it

Basically there is so much wrong with this press release that all you should do is tear it up and throw it in the wastepaper bin. That is what any responsible journalist would be inclined to do!

Admittedly, writing new contract press releases may not appear to be the most exciting aspect of media relations. But they are important and should be treated in as "newsy" a way as possible.

Why is this press release so bad?

1. There is no date of issue and no release date at the top of the page.
2. There is no further information contact named at the end of the press release.
3. Headline is nebulous, offering no essential information.
4. The whole press release is over-hyped on RMP as an organisation - the number one carrier, for example.
5. Emphasising certain key words as in MAJOR NEW - you should never indicate to a journalist what is important and what is not. That is his job.
6. Too many overstated claims on behalf of RMP - "unrivalled", "unmatched", the "best choice".
7. Too many quotes from too many sources - quotes should be used carefully and sparingly. They should never get in the way of the essential facts of the story or take prominence in their positioning in the press release.
8. Important facts are missing - what is the value of the contract? What exactly is Super 24, Super 48, Standard Service and Datapost? What, briefly, is the essential nature of ABC's business and where are they based? Where is this particular RMP distribution centre?
9. Why, when it is Royal Mail Parcels, mention the Post Office?
10. No identification of positioning or role of some spokesmen quoted.

Apart from all that, it's almost a usable press release!

Here is the alternative version:

FOR IMMEDIATE RELEASE   **15 MAY 1989**
ROYAL MAIL PARCELS WINS £150,000 ABC CONTRACT

A £150,000 contract to deliver the complete range of ABC Limited's electronic components and finished products to 2000 distributors throughout the country has been won by Royal Mail Parcels.

Taking effect from 1st June, the contract is among the largest to be run from RMP's Birmingham distribution centre and follows a three-month review by ABC Ltd into their national distribution requirements.

Because of the often delicate nature of ABC's products, which range from replacement circuit boards to desktop computers, the Nottingham-based company stipulated that the carrier would have to be able to combine fast and guaranteed delivery times with careful handling of the products and instruments.

Apart from bulk consignments to ABC's dealer network - stretching from Aberdeen to Truro - there is also a need for individual deliveries to the company's major clients, which include hospitals, electronic communication companies and local authorities.

RMP's ability to offer four distinct but integrated products together with its national distribution network was, said ABC's Managing Director, John Smith, a principal reason for awarding them the contract. The four products are Datapost, which guarantees next day delivery service before 10am, Super 24, introduced earlier this year and guaranteeing next day delivery, Super 48, guaranteeing two day service, and the Standard Service for delivery within five days.

"We shortlisted four leading parcel carriers and eventually chose Royal Mail Parcels because their own distribution network and the range of express and standard services were ideally suited to our needs. In addition, their pricing structure was the most competitive of the carriers who tendered for the contracts," said Mr Smith.

-END-

For further information:
Peter Brown, RMP District Manager
Birmingham Distribution Centre
Tel: 021 000 00000

(This version received the agency's approval).

This was judged a good press release because:

1.   Release time and date included at top of page, so the journalist knows when it was released and when he can use it.

2.   Contact name and telephone number for further information included at end of page (if sending out a press release over the weekend for use on the Monday, always include home phone number where the spokesman can be contacted).

3.   Headline encapsulates key aspects of story.

4.   First paragraphs go directly to the point, giving important details such as size of contract, brief details on customer and nature of products, importance of contract and distribution centre responsible for the contract.

5.   No hype - RMP's leading position and scale of operation is implied.

6.   Quotes do not clutter up the release and get in the way of the essential facts. In this instance, used to sum up the story.

7.   Using customer's reputation to speak "on behalf" of RMP - in other words, quality chooses quality.

8.   The mechanics of RMP's services explained briefly and in context with the customer's needs.

9.   Only one quote, at the end of the release - again using the customer to support RMP and speak on its behalf. In other words, third party endorsement.

10.   By mentioning towns such as Birmingham and Nottingham, you not only impart useful information but create the opportunity to get additional regional coverage in those areas. Secondly, by mentioning the customer's areas, there is the possibility of achieving some mentions in their trade press.

11.   Reasonable length and reasonably concise.

Mediawise, however, thinks it's still too long, and we don't necessarily share the agency's view of the value of quotes. Writing a press release is a *very* personal experience.

****

Meridian Broadcasting, one of the newer television franchises, has set up the Meridian Community Liaison Unit to help contributors with submitting ideas and programme items. Their example is not so much a press release as a report, perhaps intended for a weekly newspaper, by the chairman of a local organisation who, as far as journalistic skills are concerned, appears more keen than talented. The Liaison Unit uses numbers to identify and, after-wards, explain the errors.

Dear Sir

FORGET ME NOT CLUB (1)

The Forget Me Not Club held their meeting last Wednesday (2) and achieved a record attendance.(3) The advertised speaker, who was the clairvoyant Marjorie Woolhampton, failed to materialise due to unforeseen circumstances.(4) Helen (5) bravely took her place without any prior warning and kept us spellbound on the subject of her recent mercy dash to Bosnia (6) and the unexpected young house guests who returned with her.(7) Refreshments were provided by Gwendolen Rowridge, who treated us to one of her special fish mousses with watercress dressing and a green salad. To follow she had prepared a pavlova with an alternative of raspberry cheese cake.(8) Margaret Hannington is still in hospital (9), but is doing very well and should be out in time for the next meeting which will be at the usual time and place.(10) New members are specially welcome.(11),(12)

These are Meridian Community Liaison Unit's comments on this delicious (but sometimes all too typical) confection.

1. No headlines.
2. No date.
3. Use numbers where possible.
4. Cliches, unfortunate juxtaposition.
5. Full name - don't use initials.
6. Surely this is the main story.
7. Even more so!
8. Irrelevant.
9. Is this connected? If so, a better story.
10. Where and when?
11. How do they know where and when?
12. No contact details, name, daytime telephone.

Mediawise endorses this and other helpful advice given by the Meridian Community Liaison Unit.

****

British Red Cross has produced a useful and informative public relations handbook for its members - who are all, of course, important activists for the charity. In its handbook British Red Cross rightly encourages members to cultivate and contact their local media along the lines laid down in this book. The handbook cites a sample press release for circulation among the media in Devon.

RELEASE: IMMEDIATE   9 May 1993
LIVES WILL BE LOST UNLESS MORE PEOPLE LEARN FIRST AID SAY DEVON RED CROSS
The British Red Cross in Devon has launched an urgent appeal for more people to learn first aid. New courses will be starting at Red Cross Centres throughout the county on May 16, and the British Red Cross is urging people to attend the course and learn how to cope in an emergency. Anyone interested in attending a first aid course can find out more information and the address of their local Centre by telephoning Bill Smith on 0923 73932.

Last year only eighty-seven members of the public in Devon were trained in first aid by the British Red Cross, who are hoping that two hundred will be trained this year. The courses will run on Monday evenings from 7-9pm.

Director of the Devon Branch of the British Red Cross, Bill Smith, said "No-one knows when they might be the first on the scene of an accident, and lives will be lost unless more people learn first aid. How would you like to stand by and let a loved one die without knowing what to do?"

For further information contact:
Bill Smith
British Red Cross
Tel: 0923 73932

This constitutes informative and persuasive communication, and is ideal material on which a newspaper can base a good story.

****

The following are examples of press releases from cited sources with others where we have altered/disguised names and companies in the interests of good public relations! In your own press releases, we are confident you will not make the mistakes illustrated here. If anyone recognises his organisation or handiwork we apologise - and urge him/her to do better next time...

23 March 1993
BOOST FOR UNHAPPY HOTELS
Unhappy Hotels is reporting substantial increases in family bookings at its hotels with Terrific Times Clubs. The Unhappy Hotels at La Rochelle and Le Havre are just two hotels that have seen a dramatic growth in demand since they introduced Terrific Times Clubs at the end of last year. In particular, bookings at the La Rochelle Unhappy Hotel have grown from — — in —— to —— in ——, a —% increase. Unhappy Hotels built its first Terrific Times Club in ——, and now has 10 throughout France following an investment of over £10 million.

To stimulate further demand for those hotels with Terrific Times Clubs and maintain the current growth in the short break sector, Unhappy Hotels is offering a number of special deals:

Free separate rooms for children up to 14 years old at hotels with Terrific Times Clubs on most dates from now to the end of May.

Special midweek offers are available at all the group's French hotels....

The complete version of the press release on which this was based contained contact names and numbers, and was widely circulated to the travel/holiday trade press and travel freelances.

Again, this was a bad press release because:
1.   The plugs in the headline and first paragraph are wasted because they are too blatant, and they obscure rather than highlight the story. No newspaper or trade magazine would use a story in this form - so why send it out?
2.   The two main points - the increase in short-break holiday bookings and free accommodation for children under 14 - actually do add up to a reasonable story which, if properly presented, might appeal to the outlets that received the press release.
3.   What precisely are Terrific Times Clubs? Believe it or not, we are never told...so we end up not caring.

This would have been a more acceptable version of the press release:

23 March 1993
BOOST FOR SHORT-BREAK HOLIDAYS
Families are taking more short holiday breaks at hotels equipped with special leisure and entertainment facilities.

70

Bookings at two coastal hotels - Le Havre and La Rochelle -in the Unhappy Hotels chain, have shot up since they opened Terrific Times Clubs in January.

And the group is offering further inducements - free separate rooms for youngsters under 14 until the end of May, plus midweek discounts for the whole family....

Put that way, the story makes an immediate impact - and gets Unhappy Hotels a mention. Given added meaning and stripped of self-interest and boring statistics, it stands a better chance.

****

This time, only the first paragraph:

9 June 1993

EXTRA COMFORT FOR ELEGANT FEET

From 50's winkle pickers to classic court shoes, fashionable feet often need high heels! But elegant shoes that flatter our legs and provide extra height can be extremely uncomfortable if we spend all day on our feet. However, you no longer need to sacrifice style for comfort with the introduction of new Platform Insoles from "Kumfee", the leading footcare manufacturers.

And thus it goes on. Here we have a press release that is actually well written in bright, stylish language, which would not be out of place on a dozen or more women's pages - including the national papers. This makes it even more regrettable that the story line has been buried in a sea of inconsequential chatter. If the release is targeted mainly to smart women's pages (which it clearly is), leave the trimmings to the columnists - they do it much better. The headline's OK.

It looks better like this:

9 June 1993

EXTRA COMFORT FOR ELEGANT FEET

Insoles to take the pain out of wearing high heels will be in the shops soon.

Footcare specialists "Kumfee" are introducing a range of High Heel Insoles to combine, for the first time, comfort with style in elegant fashion shoes....

****

The third example was written not by a public relations executive but - fatally - by his client. It goes on for three pages of turgid, stilted, statistic-ridden prose. Again - although the exercise is cloaked beneath the unpromising title of "Market Update", there is a story in it somewhere. It is, of course, never allowed to get out.

30 March 1993
MARKET UPDATE
CHANGE OF FORTUNES
Over one million overseas Summer holidays were booked in January alone, which puts sales on a par with the same period in '93. February's sales were equally strong, being some 15% up on '93 and taking total sales for the two months up to over 1.8 million. Traditionally March is a much smaller month for Summer bookings, but this year has proved the most surprising month to date and we estimate it will be around 25% up on last year. In total, the first three months of this year will have produced two and a half million overseas Summer holiday bookings.

The key factors in this remarkable up-turn in market fortunes are the combination of unsettled weather, the importance the public places on their overseas holiday and the continuation of discounts by a number of high street travel retailers. In addition, the two key holiday retailers continued their TV advertising presence throughout February (and————————through-out March as well), which, by keeping holidays very much at the front of the public's mind, had a very considerable impact on bookings....

To do the author - no Hemingway he! - some justice, the piece is probably not meant to be used as such, but is intended merely to give travel writers usable material. Equally true, the facts are there, although it needs a major expedition to dig them out from what is a very long article. What it is palpably not is a press release.

30 March 1993
HOLIDAY BOOKINGS SHOOT UP
Despite the recession, family holidays abroad are selling faster than ever, with two and a half million bookings in the first quarter of this year.

January sales equalled last year's, but February was 15% up on last year, travel agents report. And March - normally a quiet month - has so far yielded three quarters of a million bookings.

"People are fed up with the gloomy economic situation and the rotten weather," said one trade source. "They see their dream holidays on TV - and they're hooked. We've brought smiles to their faces - and these days there's precious little to laugh about"....

Not perfect, but as a press release distinctly more appealing than the original. Even as pure information, it is easier to absorb than the effort of the unnamed client, who seemed altogether too inflated with his own importance to descend to the level of telling a story in a concise and readable fashion.

****

Here are opening paragraphs from three examples of jargon-infested gibberish - although to be fair they probably mean something to someone out there. All the same, they purport to be press releases, so they can be judged as that...and they do not pass the tests of clarity, conciseness and attractive presentation. Only the first release was dated, and only the third carried a contact name and phone number.

──────── ─────── ANNOUNCES NEW TEXTURED NIGHT DUSK VISUAL SYSTEM
──────── ─────── Incorporated today announced the launch of XXXXXXXX SPI/T, a new visual system that adds hardware texture to the top selling SPI either as a product or as a field retrofittable option.

Orders for the first of the new systems are expected to be announced shortly.

SPI/T is the latest in the highly successful XXXXXXXX range of computer generated image systems developed by ─────────. The range includes SP3/T, the world's first day/dusk/night system to incorporate texture capability....

Music, no doubt, to the ears of a few captive boffins at the Massachusetts Institute of Technology and the Ministry of Defence, but again, it was sent out as a press release. It's clearly hyper-smart technology - and it's British! So let's celebrate it. Unaltered, even Jane's Defence Weekly would feel compelled to rewrite. And it would probably make the average tabloid reader want to SPI/T.

****

73

Here's another example:

30 October 1993
FIFTEEN DIGITAL PABXs IN DPNSS FIRST FOR ——
——'s largest digital PABX, marketed by ——— ——— as —Tex and by —— as SLX, is the first system to demonstrate successfully that it conforms to the new United Kingdom digital signalling standard DPNSS (Digital Private Network Signalling System).

The DPNSS interface provided by the —— SLX/—Tex systems now enables the sophisticated facilities which are a feature of electronic PABXs to be extended into the digital public network. The interface utilizes a digital access signalling system (DASS) developed by ——— ——— for integrated digital access (IDA) into the —— integrated service digital network (ISDN). This is a significant step in the integration of public and private networks....

Yes, this is exactly as written, apart from the names. Once more, it is supposed to be a press release. One is bound to ask "for what section of which press?" Even if anyone understood it, would they print it in this form? What is the point of a press release - the peak of instant communication - if a journalist has to go back to its source and unravel virtually every word of it? It is obviously important: could it not have been presented in a way that actually reveals that? Our verdict: NBG.

****

On we go...
PRESS INFORMATION FOR IMMEDIATE RELEASE
COUNTERPRODUCTIVE '94 - UNRIVALLED IN EUROPE
The showcase event of the counterproductive media industry, COUNTER-PRODUCTIVE, will once again expand substantially, following the trend of recent years. What began several years ago as a small exhibition displaying the technology and applications of an infant industry, will this year be the largest in Europe, if not the world.

Demand for the exhibition space has already outstripped that for the 1993 show, with over six months still to go until the counterproductive industry once again converges on ———. Over 50 companies have already booked stands at the event, which will occupy halls One to Four at the ———....

Yet again, a press release....A press release? Six months before the event? And what can they mean - "the largest in Europe, if not the world?" Don't they know? All right, it's less impenetrable than the previous one, but written so uninspiringly. "...will once again expand substantially, following the trend of recent years..." and "...displaying the technology and applications of an infant industry..." are not terminologies likely to induce a "Phew! What a belter!" reaction on the news desk. Besides, is there a story there? So 50 companies have booked for a show six months away. If you don't relate that figure to some other (last year's total, say) it is meaningless.

****

Our next example was a press release of a speech sent out in advance and embargoed for release after the speech was made. This is a common tactic, helpful to newspapers by giving them the text in advance, and to electronic media outlets to alert them to a possible ROS (recording on site). But you still have to work at the press release: it is sloppy simply to reproduce the speech with little effort to highlight the main points and fashion them into a news story. In this release the main point came in the fifth paragraph - on page two!

"....I would go on to make a prediction - there continue to be an increasing demand for staff to engineer and maintain computer systems. The NCC has calculated that there is, already, a constant shortage of a staggering 20,000 computer staff in this country. I am now confidently stating that this demand will increase. What are we as an industry going to do about it, and perhaps more importantly what are education authorities doing about it?"

Not bad stuff - but no mention of that key figure was made, either in the first paragraph or indeed the first page. Send out the embargoed advance by all means - but don't expect the press even to turn over to page two unless you engage their attention on page one.

****

Two quickies: spot what they have in common.

9 December 1987
SUMMIT TALKS ON EDUCATION
An important breakthrough took place last week when a housing minister

and an education minister got together for the first time to discuss housing education....

15 December 1987
ENGINEERED STRUCTURES WITHSTAND THE OCTOBER STORM
The Great Storm which affected south-east England in the early morning of 16 October was the subject of an open meeting of the Institution of Structural Engineers last Tuesday, 8 December....

Answer: they are old stories. Press releases concerning events that happened a week ago qualify as documents of historical interest only. Apart from that, neither is an especially good tale....

****

Another obvious sample, as mentioned earlier, and quite famous in its way. This sale report was sent out by a firm of land agents in 1986. The headline read:

RECORD PRICE ACHIEVED FOR ONE OF ENGLAND'S MOST LOVELY SMALLER COUNTRY HOUSES

The last paragraph read:

The property....was the subject of a private sale for an undisclosed price.

We can prove it: we have the original press release!

****

Here's a really boring one.
26 October 1989
XXX XXXXXXXXX TAKES TO THE WATER
XXX XXXXXXXXX & Partners has recently completed a series of corporate identities for three interrelated firms.
When VVVVVV WWWWWWWW, a professional firm specializing in the field of water related engineering, was formed after a merger in 1993, XXX XXXXXXXXX designed an identity based on a nineteenth century

etching of Aquarius that conveyed the heritage of the merged firms and their history that stretches back for more than 100 years. Over ten years later, the successful solution has now been updated.

The water carrier remains, but in a stronger and more contemporary style, to work harder in the increasingly competitive environment of the consulting engineering business.

In addition, for VVVVVV WWWWWWWW's joint venture, construction and water engineering firm, VVVVVV QQQQQQ International, an identity has been devised that is an abstraction of rigorous construction girders with waves, to reflect the offer of the two services.

The third identity is for a new VVVVVV WWWWWWWW subsidiary. This identity features a tightrope walker, to convey the company's skill in balancing commercial and environmental considerations....

That was it, word for word. ZZZZZZZZZZ....

****

Here's one spotted by the editor of the Guardian Diary, highlighted as "Bad news, good news...".

The former Soviet republic of Georgia has been catapulted into the headlines this week as rebel forces fight to gain control of the breakaway Abkhazia region.

Eduard Shevardnadze, Georgia's president, is reported to be in retreat from Sukhumi, the centre of fierce fighting.

The Russians are understandably concerned that the trouble may overflow from Georgia into their territory.

But none of this unrest has prevented ————— Dairies from winning a significant order to ship ice cream to the Georgian capital, Tbilisi.

****

Finally, a bad case of missing the point of a story. This time it came on page three in the penultimate paragraph!

1 March 1990
CARNIVAL TIME AT BOADICEA WINE
The leaves are beginning to turn golden on vines weighed down by bunches

of grapes ripened throughout a long warm summer. Harvest time is round the corner in the Southern hemisphere and winemakers are preparing for the 1990 vintage.

That, we promise you, was the first paragraph: now turn to page three...

Boadicea Wine is the only major retail chain in the United Kingdom to offer wine from Brazil, their buyers having discovered the rounded, fruity Castel Chatelet Cabernet 1986 (£3.99 family group one shops only). For every bottle sold, Boadicea Wine is donating 30p directly to the Rainforest Foundation, a charity committed to saving the Brazilian rainforest.

Lesson One: fine writing - even when it is fine writing - is wasted in a press release. Lesson two: you have a story...and you have poured it down the sink with the sediment at the bottom of the bottle, haven't you?

Chapter 4

CONFERENCES

We shall now expand the guidelines listed earlier on Press Conferences. Press Conferences - or News Conferences, as the electronic media tend to call them - are an alternative (and still much-favoured) way to get a message across to a large journalistic audience: but as we have already warned, they can be fraught with danger.

People with only the barest knowledge of newspapermen used to claim that journalists spent their mornings deciding which was the best lunch on offer, and the afternoons sleeping it off. This was not essentially true, but it would be hypocritical to insist that it never happened, especially in the Fleet Street of 20 or so years ago, when it *was* Fleet Street. Then, the "Lunchtime O'Booze" factor was prevalent among a few hard cases in a few offices, whose day was indeed passed enjoyably enough navigating on a sea of alcohol. Like - legendarily - crime reporters, many financial specialists were notorious lunchtime drinkers, downing gin and tonics until the Stock Exchange closed and they could call it a day.

This is quite definitely not the situation nowadays. There are still national outlet journalists who will take advantage of a liquid lunch if a company/organisation/contact is unwise enough to offer it. But they are in a tiny minority: no reputable, conscientious journalist any longer expects to be entertained as of right. And without a shadow of doubt, they prefer (a) to file the story before they allow themselves to relax; and (b) to take a snack lunch which does not involve alcohol.

So going back to our roving financial specialist, you should remember that because of "Big Bang", computer communications and satellites, the money markets never close; the arena simply moves to another part of the world - but all eyes are still on it. The big banks and financial institutions may still entertain their favourite city journalists - but mineral water or orange juice are the preferred drinks...for no one knows when a money market might crash and a new front page story will have to be written.

By the same token, the much-vaunted new electronic technology and key-stroked filing/subbing/setting pioneered by Eddie Shah and embraced now by the whole of Fleet Street, has led not to later deadlines and more flexible operations, but to tighter and much earlier time-scales. An old journalist still active in 1956 has written about his early days on a regional daily newspaper in the 1880s. His practice when covering a council meeting and a magistrates' court some five miles from his base was to hire a chaise and pair, and take a friend and two young ladies with him. While he was in court, they boarded a punt on the river. There he joined them, and they berthed for a leisurely lunch, followed by a set or two of tennis. He sat through the council meeting - but rejoined his friends for dinner. Then back to the city in the chaise and pair, arriving at his office at around 11pm - still with plenty of time to write both stories and see them off the "stone" into the paper. He wouldn't be able to do that now!

It is the same in most, if not all, sectors of journalism: things happen so quickly that, even if he/she wanted to, a journalist can no longer afford to drink too much at least not while on duty or even spend too much time away from the office. It is for that reason - among others - that press conferences have to be meticulously planned. A news conference is not an excuse for a company to meet the press and entertain them lavishly, regardless of story-value.

So Give Them A Story

The journalist will expect - and is entitled to *demand* - a good news story from a press conference, and will be justifiably annoyed if misled into attending one that fails to produce a story. Journalists will not travel long distances to press conferences, unless there are very special reasons for doing so. Reporters are irritated when press conferences begin late, especially those which give a starting time that is actually used for serving coffee.

A journalist who takes maybe an hour travelling to a press conference, then half an hour while people sit around drinking coffee, followed by another hour at the news conference proper and a further hour travelling back to the office, has lost almost half the working day - and may not have a story to show for it. There are, in effect, good reasons why the press now look very carefully at press conference invitations and are much more choosy in selecting those to attend. At the end of the day, it is possible (except for the electronic media) to cover a news conference on the phone. You can talk to the organiser or principle speaker from your office, and get much the same story that you would have got had you been there.

Target The Audience

Of course, there is a difference between trying to secure space in a newspaper and deliberately targeting the specialist press. What is news in the grocery trade press is not necessarily news for the ordinary person in the street serviced by the consumer press. Ironically, though, reporters on national newspapers get many of their best stories by following up items which have appeared in trade papers and magazines. Indeed, press conferences are frequently held for selected sectors of the media, perhaps the specialist trade press or just, say, medical correspondents of the heavyweight nationals. This sort of targeting can be effective, but generally if you have a story to sell because you think it is news, you should try to attract as wide a media audience as possible.

Targeting applies not just to the outlets, but to their readerships: a new or adapted agricultural machine should be aimed not only at the principal trade papers (Farmers Weekly, Farming News, etc) but also at a handy, compressed-format magazine like "What's New in Farming?" which circulates among machinery dealers, agricultural co-operatives and other likely potential markets for the equipment.

Is A Press Conference The Answer?

But in every instance, the first decision - and the vital one -must be: do you really need to stage a press conference to launch a campaign or product which you might be able to do equally well with a simple mail-out? You can resolve this by defining the exact nature of the story you want to get across, and looking at all the possible channels for landing the story: only then should you decide whether or not a press conference really is the right vehicle.

These are the points on which you need to be satisfied:

- **is the story big enough to attract media attention?**
- **is it worth the expense of a risky news conference?**
- **are you certain there is no better alternative?**
- **if not, how are you going to put the story over?**

Having chosen a press conference as the correct medium, you have to calculate the optimum date and most convenient venue. After that, work out who is going to present it, and the strategy for (a) attracting the media;

81

and (b) landing the story. A good press conference must run without any hitches. It must be stage-managed as slickly and as professionally as a West End play. Everyone should know exactly what they have to say - and they must rehearse it so that they can deliver their lines with confidence, and so that you know precisely how long the proceedings will last. An added advantage of rehearsals - with the "dress rehearsal" in the actual venue - is that you can analyse the entire programme, and make the necessary corrections, adjustments and improvements. You can also anticipate the sort of questions that are likely to be asked, and how best to respond to them.

The timing is crucial: don't just pick a date that suits *you*: choose one that will be popular with the journalists to increase your chances of a good attendance and subsequent coverage. Make sure your event is not going to clash with another on the same subject taking place just before yours, or with a major news story that will dominate the next day's news and therefore squeeze you out, even if you do manage to attract some journalists. As previously mentioned, check dates by asking your media contacts, ringing up the diary editors of one or two newspapers, or the forward planning desk of the regional television or local radio stations.

Day And Time

Mornings are more convenient than afternoons for press conferences. Never hold an evening news conference: if anyone in your management seems to be keen on an evening conference, explain tactfully that they are not really *au fait* with media requirements. A mid morning press conference allows the journalist to go into the office first, check the mail and make or return one or two important phone calls. Furthermore, it gives the journalist plenty of time after the news conference to write copy and do any follow-up calls or interviews.

Whitehall departments often hold press conferences at 3pm or 3.30pm to coincide with the release of documents or reports in the House of Commons. Considerate journalists will appreciate that this is unavoidable: MPs should clearly not learn the contents of a White Paper through the media before the document has been presented to the House. But it is *not* a popular practice. By the time the conference is over, a reporter is under considerable pressure to write the story and get it back to the office for the next day's morning paper. This might even prove impossible, so journalists are compelled to dictate their stories - hastily written in a notebook - over the phone to a copy-taker, or transmit them (again via the phone) from a lap-top computer which inputs the material directly into the newspaper's computer system.

82

So make it a morning press call. As for the day on which you'll hold the conference, there are good days and bad days like there are good times and bad times. Some factors might apply over which you have no control, because you are always at the mercy of the day's news - and news is a fickle product. You might be able to talk round the journalist who believes he has a better story to cover - but if the Prime Minister happens to choose that particular day to resign, you are dead!

In general, though, any weekday is all right, but Tuesday, Wednesday and Thursday seem to attract better turn-outs. Monday can be lost to weekend follow-ups, and on a Friday, as we have already pointed out, coverage could well be limited because there is less space available on the news pages of the Saturday papers.

Special circumstances - particularly a powerful running story - will make evening or weekend news conferences imperative. But there you are in a crisis situation: a parliamentary vote of confidence or a released British hostage returning to Heathrow late at night clearly call for an emergency response news conference; but the story really has to be as big as that.

The bizarre craze for early morning briefings and talk-ins (based on the American presidential model of "working breakfasts") seems thankfully to be declining. Few journalists (the obvious exceptions are radio and breakfast-time television) enjoy getting up at the crack of dawn to attend one of these spurious events, and sugaring the pill with cold kedgeree, a limp croissant and warm champagne does not impress them. Public relations firms and companies thoughtless enough to inflict this on the media, should at least ensure that the champagne is served at the right temperature! A few years ago, if you held the press conference late in the morning and offered drinks afterwards, you would automatically increase the attendance; if you slotted in a buffet or sitdown lunch as well, you boosted your chances even further - although the organisers could never be sure why journalists attended their modest functions.

Indeed, during the 1980s there was a small coterie of journalists who lunched and wined extraordinarily well by attending this sort of event, and never wrote a word of copy as a result. They would scan news diaries and, through swapping information, select which would offer the best hospitality that day! Most media event organisers are delighted when any member of the press turns up, so this group rarely found it difficult to gain admsision and enjoy the free hospitality. Eventually, word must have got round on the grapevine, because organisers started checking invitations, and measures were taken to discourage this abuse. It does not happen now.

83

The Crisis Conference

Clearly, at some stage and with some strikingly important material, you might be forced to call a press conference at very short notice. This could be for a number of reasons - all coming under the general heading of crisis-handling or damage limitation (dealt with in Chapter 7). For example, such a move would be allowable to announce a product recall and calm public fears. Or possibly you want to deny serious allegations which could damage you or your company if not refuted immediately. The police frequently call hastily-convened press conferences to ask for the public's help in some way, and a hospital might summon the media at short notice in the event of a major health scare.

In these exceptional cases, faxes and telephones are your best weapons. Ring up reporters and news desks and explain why the press conference has been called at such short notice. The scent of a good story (not necessarily the sort of front-page lead referred to earlier) is all that is normally needed to secure a fair attendance.

Selecting The Venue

Choose a venue that is easy and quick to get to and from. When Fleet Street played host to most of the national newspapers, a press conference could be arranged at any one of several familiar venues in the area, with a good turnout virtually guaranteed. Nowadays, with the papers scattered throughout London, the venue is a matter of much greater importance in organising a major press conference or indeed a local one. A central London location (accessible by public transport) may be more expensive, but it means that all the journalists coming in from various points around the capital have about the same distance to travel.

Reporters in London may take taxis if they are in a hurry (and if their News Editor will pay!), but there are some parts of the capital where it is nearly impossible to get a cab back to the office, or on to the next assignment. The new Covent Garden at Nine Elms is one such area. When the market is in full swing, getting to an early news conference is just about manageable, but returning to the office is a nightmare.

Equally, there is no point in picking a deliberately unusual or off-beat venue in the hope of attracting the media if it is miles from anywhere. A press conference in the middle of a National Park may sound interesting but few journalists are going to be able to afford the luxury of spending all day travelling up and down the country. Some journalists will probably turn up, particularly those from specialist magazines interested in conservation, outdoor activities and the environment, which reinforces the need to fix precisely the sort of media attendance - and resulting coverage - for which you are looking. A former Fleet Street colleague neatly summed up his requirements for a press conference. "I want a quickie press conference, at a sensible time, with a company which has something to say and which puts the boss up to say it. Failing that I would rather have a meaningful press release and a contact able to explain and amplify it if necessary. After all, in the time taken to travel to a press conference, the press release could have been read and developed, and the copy written."

Basic Preparation

Tell your media contacts well in advance of the news conference, so that they can mark it in their diaries. You don't have to explain precisely what it is about: simply present it as a major story, so the conference will be worth their attendance. Follow this up with an invitation a week or so before the event. Again, credibility is all-important: a phone call to good contacts in the media assuring them of the news value of the conference ought to guarantee their attendance, provided (as mentioned before) that a bigger news story does not break on the day.

You cannot afford to overlook a single detail when planning the conference. These are just the first steps:

- prepare speeches and rehearse them
- produce illustrative material
- draw up a list and send out invitations
- design and produce press packs
- finalise catering arrangements.

Other important points are:

- the venue must be able to accommodate the number of people likely to attend
- it has to have the audiovisual equipment you need
- it must be able to supply a decent buffet or sit-down meal.

There will be additional considerations, but these are likely to occur to you in the course of making the general arrangements.

Presentation Strategy

Format and presentation are obviously vital. Select a key figure as chairman (he/she need not be chairman of the company) and the type of presentation guaranteed to hold maximum interest. Speakers will be required and also experts available to answer any questions that may arise from all sections of the press.

Should you want to stage a conspicuously slick audiovisual presentation, make sure you have the equipment and the experts who can operate it. To a degree, the more adventurous the presentation, the more things there are that can go wrong. Even the silliest slip-up can ruin the conference and leave your credibility and reputation in tatters. One recent major press conference fizzled out because the entire presentation was built around a slide projector show. Two minutes into the presentation, the projector bulb burnt out, and there was no replacement to be found anywhere. You can never tell when a bulb might blow, but at least there should be a spare available.

Preparation falls into three areas:
- the presentation
- the venue
- the media.

Preparation

The golden rule of the press conference is that speakers should say all they have to say in the shortest possible time. Addressing a major issue should require several speakers and a lengthy question and answer session, but you ought to be able to wrap everything up inside an hour.

The main points to follow are:
- Be absolutely clear what you intend to tell the media, and why it is newsworthy.
- Draw up a list of all the areas that need to be covered, and decide the best people to address them.
- Make sure your chosen speakers will be available on the day.
- Ensure that each speaker thoroughly prepares his/her speech.
- and that it is equally thoroughly checked.
- It is vital to pick up inaccuracies and contradictions at an early stage, and test each speech for length.
- The speeches should be clear and jargon-free.
- Do not give away any company secrets.
- Speakers should be sufficiently familiar with the material that they do not have to spend the entire presentation with

their eyes glued to the paper in front of them.
- They must be confident enough to look up and achieve eye contact with the audience.
- List all likely questions and the best responses to them.
- Work out who should answer which questions.

As long as you get the right message across and the journalists feel they have a good story, it doesn't have to be a marathon conference. Never in any circumstances drag the proceedings out unnecessarily: it will be clear to the audience that you have run out of steam - and there is a serious risk that some journalists will get up and leave before you have had the chance to sum up. They may do this anyway, not out of discourtesy but because they have other assignments.

That is why timing is so important, and why reporters appreciate it if you can tell them in advance not only the time they must come to the conference, but also how long it is likely to last. Two events in a specialist's field on one day cause a problem, usually resolved by attending one and dropping the other. But knowing they can go on from one to the other, they might be persuaded to cover both.

A simple calculation can help you make the major decision of whether or not to stage a news conference: if the whole proceedings can be dealt with in less than half an hour, then is it really worth holding a press conference at all? By the same token, if you cannot tell the story in less than, say, an hour and a half, it is better not even to try. As a compromise, stage a relatively short conference, but invite journalists to join the speakers over a drink, which does effectively extend the duration of the conference, and in a more relaxed atmosphere. Apart from these tactical considerations, the catering arrangements will be tied to a fixed point. An overrun by a few minutes is not a problem, but a badly stage-managed press conference which goes on for a long time after its scheduled finish will not only infuriate the journalists, it could ruin the lunch planned for them.

Presentation Skills

A speaker at a press conference should relate to the audience and, if possible, actually like them! Try to confine your notes to a few main headings written (or preferably typed) on cards of postcard size. Reading slowly and solidly word for word from a script, with your head down and no expression in the voice, is not the way to hold the rapt attention of the media, who will lose all interest and might get up and walk out!

87

An **autocue** (see page 90) is one solution, but it is really for the big occasion, and can appear pretentious at a modest news conference in a smallish room. Furthermore, like all props the autocue needs both rehearsal and familiarity with the technique to use it to the best effect.

Speech delivery can certainly be enhanced by learning a script by heart, but if it is a complicated presentation there is the ever-present danger of sudden memory lapses, when the speaker becomes literally lost for words. However, there are other props which can help you make an impression on the audience, and which will actually assist reporters in their note-taking. One of them is the *White Board*, an ideal medium for building a case and making bullet points in writing for all to see.

These are points to watch with White Boards:

- shield the board from light shining from a window
- start with a clean board
- use the whole board
- buy a few non-permanent pens....
- ....but pick the right ones (water- or spirit-based) - the wrong sort can ruin the board
- provide the appropriate cleaner - and spare pens
- use a point thick enough to enable everyone to see the writing clearly
- test all the pens beforehand to make sure they work
- keep the caps on the pens when not in use, to stop them drying out
- write clearly, and larger than you might think necessary
- use a combination of printing and handwriting for emphasis
- limit your writing to key points
- avoid long sentences
- keep columns straight
- stand back and check your handiwork, particularly the spelling
- pause as you write on the board
- create anticipation...
- ...with phrases like, "And the key argument..."
- use a pointer to highlight the main points
- clean the board as soon as you have finished with that part of the presentation.

NEVER...
- turn your back to the audience - except while you are writing
- doodle
- forget where you put the pen.

All these techniques apply equally to flip charts and, partly, to slides and acetates (see below).

USE THE TECHNOLOGY

Virtually any presentation at a press conference is going to be enhanced by the intelligent use of written and electronic visual aids commonly slides, overhead projections and videos. These have to be prepared, with someone delegated in charge of them. And of course, everyone has to be able to see them. The images must be clear, in focus and unambiguous or they can cause distractions. The following are the commonest and most effective visual aids.

Flip Charts

These work well with small audiences in a small room, but you still need to practise what you want to draw on a flip chart. Your writing will not be as legible to strangers as it is to your staff, and if you go into graphics or design, you could discover that you are not the ace cartoonist you obviously think you are. Check that the pages turn easily, and stay put. Pages have the habit of slipping back to their original position, so use a bulldog clip to keep them in place.

Overhead Projections

These use words and illustrations printed on acetate film. They can be projected as huge images, and drawn on while being used in the presentation. Problems include keeping the acetates separate (they tend to stick together) and placing them on the projector so that the correct image is displayed, the right way up. It is also difficult to concentrate on speaking while separating acetates that refuse to come unstuck. Unless you are adept at this, let somebody else change the acetates on cue from you. Mount the acetates in cardboard frames and keep them in protective sleeves.

Slide Projectors

These should ideally use only high-quality transparencies. Never try to cram too many into a presentation. Check the slides carefully: badly-photographed, out of focus slides are a terminal distraction. Prepare the display thoroughly and check that the slides are in the correct order, and that none is upside-down. If the slides are normally carried in a magazine or carousel, make sure the lid is secure. By using a remote device with forward/back and focus controls, speakers can themselves switch from slide to slide - but the system can go wrong, and is an extra burden that should be avoided. It is much better for someone else to operate the slide projector, using a marked script for slide changes. For sophisticated presentations, employ a specialist company which will have the equipment and skills to put on a more impressive and professional performance. Remember, slides should complement a presentation, not overshadow it; and use the same slide on a number of occasions to reinforce a point. You can achieve an extremely slick presentation and an extraordinary impact by combining two 35mm projectors and sound - but this really is the province of the specialist company operator. If you select the more modest form of presentation, establish well in advance whether it is you or the venue which is providing the necessary equipment (this applies to overhead projection as well). If it is the venue, you will be charged extra for equipment hire.

Video

Using video can really make your presentation. If it is true that a picture is worth a thousand words, then a good video is the equivalent of an encyclopaedia. Corporate or promotional videos must be professionally produced - and totally relevant. It is possible to build an entire presentation around a single piece of video, incorporating other clips to maintain pace and interest, and ancillary visual aids in support. However, you have to rehearse this sort of presentation exhaustively so that everything goes according to cue, and all the equipment works on schedule. Use of a video demands a large screen at the front of the function room, and supporting monitors strategically placed so that guests can see and hear all the time without strain. Alternatively, you could employ the latest technology and set up a massive video "wall" made up of 100 or more monitors (*very* expensive). With this you can display computer-generated graphics and split-screen presentations.

Autocues

Autocues have improved dramatically since the days of the early "teleprompter" which scrolled up the words of your speech in a slot just below the camera, enabling you to speak straight into the lens. Now an autocue can be displayed on virtually invisible glass panels or screens to your front, left and right, and a speech can even be laser-"written" in thin air so that only you can see it. Both devices are intended to give the illusion that you are speaking without notes. Most politicians now use one or the other on all major occasions. The glass panels act as television monitors, and the words of your speech appear on them at the rate at which you are speaking. It is very impressive, though if you read the entire speech from these "invisible" screens your eyes, which are focusing on the audience as well, quickly take on a somewhat vacuous appearance. So look away from time to time - or, better still, use the autocue for bullet-points to push you in the right direction, so that you no longer need large chunks of the speech written out in full. Self-evidently, this equipment needs rehearsal to master it, and is out of place at a small press conference.

Flip charts, overhead projections, slide projectors, video and autocue...these are the aids at your disposal. The size and relative importance of the news conference will dictate which combination of visual aids will suit you best. Whichever you choose, tune the equipment properly, lay in a store of spare bulbs for the projector, make sure the flip-chart stand is stable - and try not to forget the scores of other things that have to be done before you open the doors to the press.

Front Line Speakers

Nearer the day, persuade the speakers to rehearse their sections of the conference. This enables them to familiarise themselves with their own contribution, and see where it fits into the overall presentation. Discuss with speakers the points which are likely to arise from what they are going to say, and how best to answer them. Try to identify the really tricky questions that might be asked, maybe not directly as a result of the press conference, but perhaps because of the speaker's involvement in a particular industry sector. You could have called the conference to announce a totally safe organic pesticide, yet your key speaker might still end up being questioned about the industry's general pesticide record. This is an almost inevitable line of questioning from a journalist with a strong track record as an environmental lobbyist.

The best physical format to adopt for a news conference involving complex presentation is a long table (covered to the floor) on a slightly raised platform at one end of a rectangular room, facing rows of chairs divided by a wide

91

central aisle (for visual aid equipment and television cameras). There you will seat the conference chairman and, ideally, no more than four speakers. Each must have a clearly legible name card.

If you have structured the conference properly, there will be time for a *five-minute* presentation by the conference chairman setting out the principal theme and introducing the speakers; followed by *no more than ten minutes* from each speaker, making the presentation with visual aids. Then comes the questions session, and lastly a brief wind-up.

The speakers must include the Chief Executive (whether Chairman or Managing Director) of the company/organisation. The press will expect to see the top person there, exposed to questioning. A typical conference called to present, say, plans for a new plant which will bring jobs and prosperity to your home base city, should feature:

- **The Chief Executive** - to set out the broad principle and impact of the proposed new factory
- **The Technical Director** - to explain the function of the building, its technology and advantages over the existing plant
- **The Sales Director** - to present home/export figures and future projections
- **RESIST** the temptation to import a political/show business celebrity to give the presentation "star" quality. This will be seen as pure artifice, and will waste valuable time. An exception could be made if the "celebrity" is actually associated with the company, organisation or cause.

No speech should exceed its stated length: no question should be evaded, within the limits of company/industrial discretion. If you have to evoke confidentiality, do it light-heartedly, and with a proper explanation of why you are unable to provide a precise answer.

The Press Pack

One duty will be to design and supply press packs which the journalists take away with them, or which can be sent to those members of the media who, for whatever reason, failed to turn up. It should contain:

- a press release explaining what the conference is about
- copies of all speeches
- photographs of the speakers
- usable pictures of the new product or building

- background information to expand the press release into a feature
- contact name and telephone numbers.

Type Of Venue

The hotel or meeting-rooms where you decide to hold the event will be far more used to hosting press conferences than you are, so take the advice of the functions or banqueting manager. Choose a room of sensible proportions: you won't want the ballroom if you are expecting only half a dozen journalists; equally embarrassing is a room which is far too small. If you are going to serve coffee before the presentation or drinks afterwards, you will need two adjacent rooms; even a light buffet lunch can be an unpleasant experience if there are not enough chairs for everyone to sit down while they eat.

The chairs in the press conference room itself must be comfortable and individual, rather than linked. Hard chairs cause people to shuffle about and lose concentration, while chairs that are joined together in rows make it difficult for latecomers to take their places with the least disruption. Arrange for extra chairs - but not too many. While you should budget for unexpected arrivals, it is disconcerting for speakers to see row upon row of empty seats and reflects badly on the organisers, since guests will assume that you expected far more people to attend.

If there is a reasonable attendance, but a lot of room at the front, resist the temptation to try to persuade people to move forwards to fill up an empty row. Journalists don't like sitting in the front rows at any function: they prefer to be seated at the back, from where they can make an easy escape.

Of course, the room should be suitable for a presentation of the type you wish to stage. That means no pillars to obstruct anyone's view, and no large, uncurtained windows looking out on to a street. Avoid basement rooms that lie directly over an underground railway line.

Check the room lighting to ensure that you can dim and raise the lights without having to flick a battery of switches each time. Emphasise that the room must be isolated from the hotel's piped music and public address systems. It is frustrating for a speaker to be interrupted by the tannoy paging a hotel guest. Check that the air-conditioning can be switched off: a noisy unit can obliterate a soft speaker.

Obviously, the presentation area should be attractive, well-lit and fully-equipped. A large room should already be wired with a sound system - but may not be. This is one of the details you have to check when you make the booking: finding out at the conference itself that there isn't a sound system is leaving matters injudiciously late! And of course, test the system fully before the conference gets under way.

Again, if it is a big room, you may need roving microphones so that journalists can ask questions, and everyone else can hear them. Speakers may use fixed or clip-on microphones, or neckmikes, but they should go through a familiarisation process to find out how each type works. They must appreciate, for instance, that if they are using a fixed microphone at a lectern, it will not pick up their voice if they turn away to discuss a slide which has just appeared on the screen behind them.

Accomplished speakers may not require notes and often like to move around the platform; those less confident will prefer hiding behind a lectern. Some even read their lines from an autocue, though this is not recommended for most press conferences.

Ask the venue to supply a jug of water, or some other soft drink, and glasses for the speakers. A properly equipped conference room will have desks, or some other solid surface, for participants to use to take notes. Most hotels will not be able to provide these facilities - but the least you can do is place a notepad and presentation pen on each chair; the reporter will then have something to write with if his own pen runs out, and somewhere to rest a notebook.

It is also good tactics to set up a check-in desk for identification labels and any other information you are handing out at that stage. The desk can be either outside the room where the press conference is taking place, or just inside the door. Ask the journalists to sign a register: it is important to know who is there, and also who has failed to show up, so that you can send the non-attenders a press pack. A reporter who made every effort to come to the conference but was prevented at the last moment is as likely to give you publicity as one who actually attended. Cloakroom and toilet facilities should be nearby - and, above everything, make absolutely certain that there are telephones and at least one fax machine available for the media to use. If there is none handy, it will be worth the expense to have a number of BT/Mercury lines installed in a neighbouring room.

Ask the venue management to signpost the conference and, if it is in an hotel, to station someone at Reception who knows where the conference is being held. If you are expecting a television crew, tell the management because the crew's arrival could be disruptive. If a celebrity is taking part in the press conference, you must ensure that the venue's security staff are aware of this. Should it be a member of the Royal Family or a Cabinet minister, Scotland Yard Special Branch will already have been in touch with them, and you, to approve the arrangements.

Media Invitations

Draw up an invitation list using your media file and other sources we have mentioned, and mail the invitations out in good time. You could even risk (as already mentioned) sending each potential media invitee a "teaser" note a month ahead asking them to try to keep a particular date free for your event. No further details need be supplied at that stage.

With the invitation itself, it is a good idea to include a reply-paid slip to fill out and return. This will indicate whether they will attend and, if not, who will represent them; and if they do intend to come, whether they will be staying for lunch or drinks.

A week or so before the event, contact all the invitees. Ask those who didn't reply if they are coming, and to those who did reply, say how much you are looking forward to seeing them -stressing that you have a good story lined up.

Much could depend on the invitation, journalists receive a great many - how do you ensure that yours is the one they accept? Here are a few suggestions:
- **Lay the ground with the "teaser" as outlined above**
- **Stress in the invitation that you will provide a strong and immediately usable news story**
- **Let the timetable show them that you will take up only an hour to an hour and a half of their time...**
- **...but with the important addition of a lunchtime finish and lunch if they want it.**

The "teaser" should go something like this:
October 2, 1993
Dear ———,
I am contacting you with an early warning of a good story coming out of a news conference on Wednesday, 3 November. It is a story you would not want to miss.

This notice is going to your News Desk and Picture Desk as well, so that they can pencil it in the diary. But the invitation, when it comes in about a fortnight, will be to ask you specifically if you can cover the news conference.

If you know already that you will not be free on that date, or perhaps away from the office, please let me know as soon as you can so that I can make alternative arrangements.

Kind regards

THE INVITATION WILL, OF COURSE, BE EXPLICIT

14 October 1993

Dear ————,

Thank you for letting me know you'll be available to cover our news conference on 3 November. You won't regret it. We are going to make an important announcement which will affect the prosperity of the city, and the jobs and futures of a great many people living here.

The venue is the Fordyce Suite at The George Hotel, Market Street. The timetable is as follows:

1100: Assemble for coffee
1115: News conference opens
1120: Main presentation by Astrolex executives
1200: Questions
1230: Wind-up
1235: Drinks
1245: Buffet lunch

A place has already been reserved for you in the car park at the rear of the hotel. A telephone - with Tandy connection -and fax machine will be provided.

I do hope you will be able to make it. To help us finalise our strategy and catering arrangements, I enclose a reply slip and prepaid envelope.

Kind regards

REPLY SLIP

NAME...

NEWSPAPER/MAGAZINE/BROADCASTING OUTLET
....

I WILL/WILL NOT BE ABLE TO ATTEND THE ASTROLEX NEWS CONFERENCE AT THE FORDYCE SUITE, THE GEORGE HOTEL, MARKET STREET, ON 3 NOVEMBER (Please cross out as applicable).

I WILL BE REPRESENTED BY.................................

I WILL REQUIRE A FIRST-CLASS RETURN RAIL TICKET FROM.. ...

I WILL/WILL NOT STAY FOR LUNCH

If the press conference is being held at an unusual venue, or out-of-the-way place, it is a good idea, a few days beforehand, to supply an easy-to-read map. This is another way of jogging their memories about the event, as well as helping them find it. Prepare media badges showing journalists' names and which organisation they represent. Use different coloured badges to distinguish between your own staff, the media, and other guests. Name badges help break the ice: you might have spoken to someone many times on the phone without ever meeting them; the badge puts a face to the name.

You will need one or two people to man the press desk, welcoming journalists and asking them to sign the register. Other people from the press office/public relations staff should mingle with the journalists before the press conference gets under way, answering queries, noting special requests, and making everyone feel at home. As conference organiser and, for most people, principal contact, you will perform the dual role of greeting as many guests as possible, while ensuring that everything is running smoothly behind the scenes.

Press packs should not ideally be handed out until the end, although there will always be one or two journalists who feel more comfortable with the information in front of them before the conference starts. Your own photographer will be on hand to take pictures of the speakers and of anything else required. As previously advised, the press pack should contain the main press release, copies of the speeches, and brief biographies and photographs of the speakers.

Journalists will use your inscribed pen as soon as they sit down, and it is a reasonably common practice to include a small gift with the press pack they get when they leave. This is by no means necessary - and the gift must not be valuable. On the other hand, if the press conference is staged to announce the launch of a new food product, or some easily portable computer gadget, then it is quite acceptable that you should want media guests to have a sample as a present.

But a careful balance has to be drawn between what is considered suitable as a gift, and what might be construed as an inducement. A number of newspapers have adopted the policy that their staff will not accept anything in the way of gifts or samples, in case it may be seen as trying to influence what they write. You will want to spare recipients the embarrassment of having to "declare" their present to the news desk for assessment as a possible bribe!

Pre-Conference Check List

Arrive in good time to ensure that everything is arranged as you want it. Ask your speakers to come early as well. If necessary, book them into the press conference hotel (or one nearby) the night before the conference so that if they do oversleep, they are still somewhere close at hand.

Lay out the press desk, put up any posters or promotional material, and check that the location of the press conference is clearly marked. Finalise the catering arrangements, test the microphones and visual presentation equipment one last time, make certain that your own staff have no serious problems - and then take a well-earned break before the journalists arrive. Once that starts to happen, everything steps up a gear. Try to keep to your published timing, unless there is a very good reason for delaying. If you have laid on coffee for the media in a side room, start to usher them into the press conference venue a few minutes before the designated start, and alert your speakers.

Who's In Charge?

You will already have chosen a chairman: as we have hinted, this can be a ticklish process. Being Chairman or Managing Director of a company is a very different function from presiding over a news conference. The Chief Executive will in any case be there as the chief corporate representative of the company, and should have a specific role to play - but not, in our opinion, as chairman of the news conference. Should this create difficulties, explain that this is a media, not a corporate, occasion.

We have no hesitation in advising that the ideal chairman of the press conference is the person who organised it: you. The role of conference chairman is, after all, largely ceremonial: welcoming guests, introducing speakers, selecting questions. That third function is the most crucial: you want to head off awkward questions and persistent questioners. Who better to do this than the only person on the platform that actually *knows* the reporters? Only *you* are in a position to control the conference properly, because - as chief press officer, head of public relations, director of public affairs...whatever your title - you know the journalists' idiosyncracies and obsessions. The task of conference chairman is all about control. You know beforehand that whatever the subject of the conference, a certain correspondent will always try to find out how much everything costs; another is obsessed with benefits to consumers; a third with safety aspects.

Only you at the top table can identify these people and control the flow of questions so that everyone who wants a turn gets one, and nobody is allowed to belabour his pet topic to the point of tedium. No-one else can perform this job as effectively as you can: it rests with you to insist that no-one else does.

Conference Presentation

The conference must follow your prearranged ground plan:
- welcome the media, and thank them for coming
- outline briefly what the occasion is about
- introduce the speakers and the areas they will cover
- launch straight into the speeches
- followed by a controlled question and answer session
- and finally the wind-up.

Stick to the game plan and timings. Only you, as chairman, will know the internal timings - how long each speaker is scheduled to run, for example - and it is up to you to exercise the necessary pressure to keep matters on course. If everything goes well, there will be a stream of questions from journalists. If you have given birth to a damp squib, there will be a deafening silence. You will, of course, have prepared for this (which might be nothing more serious than a slow start) by planting questions in the audience to get things moving. The "plants" should be sympathetic journalists, not members of the company. Most journalists, if they are reasonably good contacts, will be prepared to accommodate you in this small respect. The tactic usually works in triggering further questions - so you have a real press conference well under way.

Once the questions start drying up, move towards a close rather than endure an embarrassing silence. The summary should in any case begin about five minutes before the scheduled end of the event. It will take the form of a brief resume of the project/product, and the points that have been made, by speakers and questioners alike. It will end with your thanks to the journalists for attending, and an invitation to join you for lunch/drinks, and a more relaxed contact on a less formal basis with the company's executives. Most journalists will have other jobs to cover or other things to do, but there will always be one or two who hang around to the bitter end. Don't be too impatient about getting rid of people. The chances are that you have booked the room for a certain period, so you have the excuse of incurring extra charges which will help encourage stragglers to leave.

Back in the office, arrange for press packs to be sent to all those journalists who didn't turn up, and to attend to any special requests you may have had during the conference. A journalist on a trade magazine, for instance, could require some special statistics, and you must ensure these are sent promptly. A quick response will impress the journalist, who will note your reliability; if you forget to do it, or deliberately ignore the request, the journalist might well not bother to get in touch with you again.

Bear in mind that the news story you have announced is going to attract media attention. Journalists who could not attend the press conference may want phone interviews; television stations may contact you with requests to film your factory at work; radio reporters who did not attend, or did not manage to get an interview with the right contact at the conference, will try again. In fact, if the conference has been successful and a Press Association story is already out on the wire, you could have to deal with a lot more media inquiries - so be prepared.

A "debriefing" session a week later is another recommended sequel: by then you will know how successful the event was in terms of copy produced, and what lessons you and the company have learned from it.

Follow-Up Stories

Your media strategy must include a good follow-up story: a really successful press conference attracting a lot of publicity provides even more justification for following it up quickly. Take a purely local example of a conference called to announce a charity appeal to raise funds for the local hospital. A follow-up press release would say how successful the launch had been, how much money had been raised, or how the money was to be spent. The papers that used the original story will carry the follow-up, and some may even claim that the resulting success was due directly to the publicity they had given it. Whether this is true or not is immaterial, provided you get the additional publicity you are seeking.

How Not To Do It!

Occasionally press conferences go dreadfully wrong. This is especially so if the initial premise is wrong: in other words, you are holding a press conference you would have been much better advised not to hold.

There are, sadly, quite a few examples: a press conference was called some time ago by a big public relations company which had won a lucrative contract to promote a particular sector of the meat industry. Journalists were deluged with phone calls and invitations to attend a champagne breakfast press briefing at which, they were assured, a major announcement would be made about the industry's future.

The attendance was surprisingly good - and the press took their places only to hear speaker after speaker talk about the history of the industry, its critics, its problems - in fact, every conceivable topic *except* its future. Certainly nothing remotely newsworthy. It was one of the rare occasions where journalists walked out, not just because they had been lured into attending, but because they had much better things to do with their time. The public relations company retained the account for a couple more years but it lost the respect of a great number of journalists. More damagingly, the meat sector it "represented" developed an extremely jaundiced view of both the media and public relations.

Press Briefings

A press briefing, instead of a full-scale press conference, can be a very effective - even superior - way of reaching the media and establishing contacts. Of course, the same stipulation applies: you hold a press briefing only if you have something worth saying.

Briefings proliferate in the weeks before a Budget, as different industry groups invite journalists to meet them to discuss what the Chancellor might or might not do. The drinks industry for instance holds a briefing to warn against putting more tax on alcohol. The journalists usually print some sort of story, and the industry hopes that the resulting publicity might have some influence at the Treasury. The industry is right in one respect: the stories are certainly seen, and duly noted.

There is no doubt that a carefully-scheduled press briefing, well-timed and attracting the right journalists, can be very successful. Correspondents in all specialisations - lobby, diplomatic, crime, industry - who report directly on the activities of the Government are constantly being summoned to briefings by ministers and civil servants. There are lobby and Foreign Office briefings every day - sometimes twice a day.

The briefing is a favourite tactic with ministers who want to test the water for a tricky piece of legislation or potentially unpopular benefit cut. By deliberately leaking the news themselves, they can judge public response - and decide on that basis either to go ahead or shelve the project. The "planned tax increase" (a favoured subject for this kind of treatment) may never actually have been in prospect at all! However, the briefing will give ministers and their advisors a penetrating insight into what reaction to expect if they ever did seriously consider such a plan. The briefing will involve only a small number of carefully selected journalists, and usually takes place in an informal atmosphere. It can even be "one to one" between a minister or industrialist and an influential correspondent, but briefings work better with three or four senior journalists. The non-political briefing will generally include one representative from each media sector (national newspapers, trade journals, radio and television). In this way individual requirements can be met, and the journalists will not have to compete with each other, since their story requirements are likely to be different.

The political or diplomatic press briefing is always on a strictly unattributable basis. This does not mean that the material cannot be used - publicity, after all, is the purpose of the briefing - but simply that quotes must not be ascribed directly to people. The correspondent will deal in terms of "Whitehall sources"..."sources close to the Prime Minister"... "sources close to the Royal Family"..."industry leaders"... "informed sources..." etc. The general public is sophisticated enough to realise that the message actually is coming from the Trade Minister or Chancellor, the Prime Minister, the Queen - or simply "the Government".

The non-political briefing can adopt the same "unattributable" status, but normally does not. So the chairman of the company and chief executive, or their equivalents, might host a briefing where a clearly-signalled part of the proceedings is "on the record", while other material is "off the record":

again, this does not mean that it cannot be used, simply that it must not be attributed in direct quotation.

If it is an industrial briefing, try to get your top people there, as long as they do not outnumber the journalists. Equal numbers on each side are acceptable, so that one-to-one conversations are encouraged. Briefings can take place in the company's board room, or in the Chairman's or Minister's private office, or over lunch in a restuarant - the more relaxed the atmosphere, the more comfortable everyone is going to feel. But always lay down clearly established ground rules: and don't get carried away. However relaxed and confidential the occasion, you are still talking to journalists - so be careful what you say. Just because you are enjoying a glass of malt whisky and a smoked salmon sandwich with a journalist doesn't mean that you can trust him.

Press Visits

Other facilities useful for attracting media attention and subsequent publicity include the press visit. Press visits can be arranged to almost any type of industrial or commercial undertaking, provided there is something to see or interesting people to meet.

For a wine importer, it is generally a good idea to take a small group of selected journalists to visit the vineyards of some of your key producers. If they are shown - and sample -exceptional wines, they will write about them, and the costs of the trip will be more than covered by increased sales generated by the positive publicity.

A manufacturer whose industry has been criticised for poor standards might well arrange a press visit so that journalists can see for themselves. Apart from the publicity, you should develop lasting media contacts. In some cases it might be better to invite a single journalist, rather than a group. Offering a journalist an "exclusive" is tempting, and there is a better chance of publicity if the journalist can persuade his paper or magazine that they have the story to themselves.

Another rewarding tactic is the familiarisation visit. A new agriculture correspondent, for example, could be taken to see how a big farm operates. This can be mutually beneficial: you will get to know a valuable contact on your own ground, and the new correspondent, who has much to learn about his subject, will be grateful for the opportunity to do so.

Float the idea of a press/familiarisation visit, and gauge the likely response. Find out what the press would like to see, and whom they wish to meet. If the reaction is positive, select your group and arrange a convenient date.

Follow this up with the actual invitation, setting out all the information they will need.

On either type of visit (or, as we have noted, for an actual press conference) journalists may choose to travel by train, in which case you will supply train times and arrange to meet them at the station, and send them first class return rail tickets. If you can, compress the visit within a single day, allowing time for the journalists to return to their offices.

There are many good reasons for organising press visits as an alternative or supplement to a press conference. It doesn't matter as long as the occasion is genuinely newsworthy. Once the journalists are there, you can show them at first hand what your business is about - and mix that business with pleasure. Follow a factory or farm tour with an informal lunch. It doesn't have to be an elaborate affair: you can lunch in the works canteen or in a local pub, as long as it gives you and the journalist the chance to get to know each other in a relaxed atmosphere.

Other Opportunities

Should you be looking for reasons to involve the press in your business, don't neglect ceremonial occasions like boardroom dinners or annual meetings. Making the press welcome at a semi-private social occasion can be a persuasive strategy. Exhibitions, or appearances at shows, provide useful opportunities if you can come up with a good news angle. And make sure there is a follow-up story for the trade press about the business you obtained through the exhibition/show.

Conferences And Seminars

These provide excellent opportunities for attracting the media and securing publicity. Send a comprehensive programme out with the invitation: specialist magazines may want to cover the whole proceedings, but national journalists are likely to be interested only in the main speaker. Most seminar programmes contain a section to be filled out by applicants for places at the event and conference meals. If it is not too much trouble, include a separate invitation for the press: a seminar can cost hundreds of pounds for a place. News desks must not be given the impression that their specialist has to pay. Treat the seminar like a press conference as far as arrangements are concerned: reporters will not ask questions, but they want to know the full names of those who do put questions. And you could easily make key speakers available to the press for an impromptu news conference. You will, of course, supply copies to the press of all papers to be read at the seminar:

it might annoy other guests, but it will save the journalists a great deal of time -particularly when (as most seminar organisers invariably do) you turn down the lighting to accommodate the visual aids. How, then, can you reasonably expect a reporter to take notes? Don't neglect the opportunity for providing your own publicity: if the Press Association, say, is not represented at the seminar, write a short news report and phone it over during the lunch hour. Then file another at about 4pm. Do the same for papers like the Financial Times and the Daily Telegraph in case the Press Association drops the story.

You don't have to depend on a specially organised seminar to generate favourable publicity. Always be on the alert for potential news stories, and if you think you have a good one, tell the media about it.

Chapter 5

THE ELECTRONIC MEDIA: RADIO AND TELEVISION

Here is a scenario - fictional, but regrettably typical of the way many top people from industry and even politics approach a television interview. The interviewee, of course, is convinced he knows everything there is to know about appearing on the electronic media. The last thing he will need is...*training?*

Scene: a television studio, cosily set (armchairs, antique occasional table, twin water carafes, matching crystal glasses, Watteau print, sympathetic curtains) for a consumer programme. Cut to panoramic view, showing two fixed, remote-controlled cameras, plus one mobile. Zoom in on earnest, bespectacled presenter, introducing a guest previously seen lounging in profile. The guest visibly straightens up, leans forward (going out of shot), barks "What?", and leans back. The presenter is saying "....Fanshaw, who is managing director of...." Cut to guest tightening his tie rather too efficiently, then loosening it again. The tie is blue; so is his shirt, with narrow white stripes.

FANSHAW: Actually, it's chairman and chief executive...

(Cut to presenter). I'm terribly sorry, did I

FANSHAW: Yes, you did. (A caption appears from telecine: Ethelbert Fanshaw, Managing Director. The stripes of Fanshaw's shirt ripple disconcertingly; his name undulates slowly across his tie).

PRESENTER: What, then, is your response, Mr Fanshaw, to what, after all, is an unmistakable attack on the way you do business?

FANSHAW: Well, of course, the whole thing's been got up by the press...wildly exaggerated, twisted out of all proportion.

PRESENTER: There's no truth in it whatsoever?

FANSHAW: Absolutely none. And I want to make clear that we are consulting our company lawyers, and

106

PRESENTER: Two children died, Mr Fanshaw; one of them a handicapped baby.

FANSHAW: Not from using our products   and I hope you're not suggesting -

PRESENTER: I don't have to suggest anything, Mr Fanshaw. The inquest made it quite clear they were using your products when

FANSHAW (spluttering and twisting in and out of shot): I'd better warn you to be very careful before you accuse me or my company of anything. There's such a thing as legal redress.

PRESENTER (smoothly, completely at ease): I take you at your word, Mr Fanshaw. As it happens, I haven't accused you, or your company, of any misdemeanour, or neglect, or malpractice of any description. As far as I can see, you've just done that very neatly for yourself.

The interview crackles and limps to its inevitable conclusion: comprehensive defeat for the guest.

Exaggerated? Perhaps, but not greatly. All the basic mistakes made by "Fanshaw" have been committed to some degree by people who have called Mediawise in to give them electronic media training -in other words, teaching them the techniques of being interviewed on television and radio. The scenario illustrates that there is a right way and a wrong way to conduct oneself in an interview. Fanshaw not only got it wrong: he broke every rule in the book.

True, the presenter gave him the wrong title, but in correcting this, Fanshaw came across as pedantic and self-important. Any audience sympathy he may have had he forfeited at that point; it is almost impossible to regain it in a three minute interview. He wore all the wrong clothes and generated a strobe effect, which will have further distracted viewers. Fanshaw had not prepared for the interview (unforgivable in view of the seriousness of the subject matter).

Rather than defend his company with reasoned and persuasive arguments, he chose to bluster and threaten. It was nigh on suicidal to accuse the press of a vindictive campaign, because the interviewer is, after all, a journalist. Fanshaw did have a case to answer, otherwise he would not have been invited to do the interview, but he wasted every opportunity to defend or justify the actions of himself and his company.

Instead, he lost his temper - and this, without doubt, is the most dangerous thing you can do while being interviewed. The interviewer is the professional and will tie you up in knots as soon as you lose control of the situation.

Assuming Fanshaw kept his job after his appalling performance, he should

107

have contacted a media training company as soon as he got back to his office, and signed up for an intensive course. This chapter, we hope, will explain what radio and television interviews are all about, and help equip you to handle them.

Basic Strategy

We shall offer detailed advice on interview strategy and tactics later in this section, but there are a few key points to observe which can be dealt with briefly here.

Don't be afraid to lay down ground rules about what you are prepared to discuss. If you have something to hide, the interviewer is going to try to ferret it out, but he/she will appreciate that there is no point in asking you about something of which you have no knowledge, or have no authority to discuss.

The interview setting - in a studio or on location - can be important for you. Choose the live interview if it is appropriate -it is always preferable, because you can say anything you wish to say in a live interview. On the other hand, a location interview might be more relevant. A press officer of a conservation group leading a protest against plans to destroy an ancient woodland, would prefer to record the interview - whether it is radio or television - in front of the woods that are threatened. There are situations, however, when you should be on your guard when a television reporter suggests interviewing you at your place of work. For instance, if your company is being criticised locally for causing pollution, it does your case no good at all to be interviewed alongside an outfall pipe spewing waste into the river, or in front of the factory chimney belching out black fumes.

RADIO

Radio and television are an essential part of our national life, and play an increasingly important role in it. Major issues are now often fought and won over the air waves rather than in Parliament, board rooms, even the courts. A good "performance" can reap enormous dividends - a bad interview can be disastrous.

Listeners are counted in millions 24 hours a day, seven days a week, all through the year. BBC Local Radio alone averages nine million listeners a day. Radio's appetite for material is voracious. Broadcasters are always eager for stories and interviews to fill current affairs or "mixed" programmes, and they want them, wherever possible, straight from the people most involved those who have direct experience of the subject under discussion.

This demand should be welcomed, and one should do everything possible to encourage it. There are enormous opportunities for broadcasting, especially on radio, and even greater benefits if you do it well. A good interviewee can turn a hostile audience into a sympathetic one, and he/she can get across a message that would have cost tens of thousands of pounds to advertise, as well as establishing credentials as a regular performer.

Are You The Right Person To Do The Interview?

This is the first question you should ask yourself. Obviously, if you are a security guard at the factory gate, it will not be your job to answer questions from the media. Equally, it doesn't always follow that the company chairman or chief executive is the best person either. All companies, organisations and societies should appoint someone whose task is to handle the media. But there are special requirements when it comes to dealing with radio. First of all, you need someone who is able to perform on the media. It is surprising how many people immediately freeze as soon as they are confronted with a microphone, and cannot speak a word. This is hugely embarrassing for the programme presenter as well as the interviewee - and, more crucially, it wastes a golden opportunity to get a message across. The spokesperson must know what to say and how best to say it, *and* how to field tricky questions.

All spokespersons who deal with the media on a regular basis should have media training, but confidence comes only with practice - and no amount of practice can quite match actual experience. Experience will also teach you to recognise and side-step questions designed to trap you into an unwary admission, or lead you in a direction you would rather avoid. For radio, the ideal spokesperson is the one who comes across best. While company chairmen or managing directors may think they are the only people equipped to handle a media interview, if they appear to be arrogant, hectoring or pompous, or simply speak softly - or too loudly - they can actually be doing the company a disservice by appearing. Since many people listening to the radio are normally doing something else (such as housework or driving), it is important to engage their attention straight away and hold on to it. So the choice of spokesperson has to be made with extra care. In large companies, it is obviously useful to have a team of executives who have been media-trained.

When You Are Asked To Appear...

Generally speaking, always accept the offer of a broadcast interview. It is free publicity - and even if it were possible to buy space in programme time, you couldn't afford the asking price. So agree to the interview, but only after you have checked a few important points. Clearly, you must know why the programme wants you, and what they expect you to talk about. You could encounter the first pitfall at this stage: the programme might have discovered something about you or your organisation which they want to pursue, but which you would prefer to keep confidential. The decision is then up to you. You can take part in an effort to limit the damage, or refuse to participate, in which case the reporter or programme presenter will certainly reveal that fact in the context of the item which the programme will, in any case, do - with or without your co-operation.

Even if you are the official spokesperson, you should resist the offer to do an immediate telephone interview straight into a programme or news bulletin. This is not *necessarily* a tactic designed to trap you - but avoid it all the same. Make an excuse and promise to ring the reporter back in a few minutes. You could say that the building's fire alarm system is due to be tested any second, and that would wreck the interview. Even if you are experienced at giving interviews, and know exactly what you would say, it is always advisable to give yourself a little preparation time. Instant, off-the-cuff reactions can land you in a lot of trouble. Instead, give yourself a little time to collect your thoughts, and jot down the two or three important points that you want to make.

It is sensible to check with the company's press or public relations officer to make sure that (a) they know what is going on, and (b) that what you plan to say is the company line. It is also conceivable that the reporter who phones you may know something about a particular situation that you have not yet been told. The press office may know it, too, so by contacting them you will get all the information you need. Most situations, however serious, are unlikely to be affected by postponing an interview for ten minutes or so. If the reporter misses the 11am news bulletin, the item can still be slotted in for the 11.30am summary or the next bulletin at noon.

Most telephone interviews will be short because of the indifferent broadcasting quality. In a news bulletin, they rarely last for more than 15 seconds. Even in a programme, with an interview that could not be obtained by any other means, efforts will be made to record a telephone interview to select only the most important segments. The exception is, of course, the "phone-in" programme - but that is not the type of programme we are discussing here. Phone-in programmes are popular because they are arguably the cheapest form of broadcasting in existence. They should not be ignored, but they do not represent ideal publicity.

Preparation

An experienced media spokesperson will already have on file a number of "position statements" covering a variety of crisis situations. These will be available as holding statements in response to practically any emergency. Assuming that you are engaged in sensitive areas, it is a good idea to have statements prepared justifying your position in case you are criticised. The advantage of "position statements" is that by preparing them in advance, you can also identify the difficult questions you might be asked about them. Another advantage is that when a crisis arises, you already have a statement which can be released immediately; in general, the faster one responds to a crisis the greater the possibility of successful damage limitation.

Furthermore, if you have distributed the position statements to all those people who might be involved in crisis handling, you will speak with a common voice. It is surprising, and frightening, how few companies prepare adequately for emergencies, and how many company spokespeople are not able to say succinctly just what it is that their company does. Indeed, if you ask two or three people in the same company the same question, the chances are you will get different answers.

One of the purposes of media training is to try to prepare a company - not merely its spokesperson - to face the media. That is why position statements are useful: they focus thinking in advance, and establish a unified response.

In a critical situation, your company might well be contacted by several radio stations and you will need to be able to field a team of trained spokespeople. It is imperative they all know and follow the company line.

By crystallising your thoughts, you can prepare "bullet points" which succinctly and effectively get the messages across. These points should never be learned parrot-fashion because when delivered they will sound hollow, but they should be so familiar to you that you can deliver them with authority and conviction.

A company which is constantly meeting the media should produce a booklet of the questions most commonly asked, and then work out the appropriate answers - and how best these should be framed. Impress upon the members of your interview team the necessity to develop bullet points, and practise interviews whenever they get the chance. Either standing in front of the bathroom mirror or alone in your car, practise your lines. The question and answer booklet will also cover the worst questions you could be asked - and will list the correct responses.

But regardless of the amount of preparation, it is still possible to be caught out. That is why it is so important to find out the precise ground an interview will cover. You might be able to get hold of new statistics to counter arguments made against you if you have an idea what those arguments will be. If you are taking part in a studio debate with someone who opposes your views, you can search out a damaging quote they have made which undermines their position or shows that, in the past, they actually supported your view.

Intelligent preparation will include consulting other experts to get the latest views, but be sure to differentiate clearly between information given purely for background briefing purposes, and points that can safely be made public. After all, you do not unwittingly want to give away company secrets.

As well as establishing your own ground rules, you are required to play by those of the broadcaster. You should anticipate two basic types of question, especially in the limited format of a news bulletin or fast-paced "mixed" programme. The first approach will ask for information, or try to find out if a particular situation or action has taken place or is planned; the second seeks a reaction to an already accomplished fact.

For instance, a reporter might ask "Why is your company planning to make 250 people redundant?" or "Why has your organisation pulled out of the local sports tournament?", which are "action" questions. The equivalent "reaction" questions would be "Are you happy about the decision to...?" or "What do you plan to do about...?"or simply "What is your reaction to the news that...?"

The Tactical Approach

There is every reason why a company should try to initiate rewarding publicity as well as trying to limit the damage caused by hostile stories. Do not feel that your opportunities for enhancing the company's image are restricted to big events and national stories. Every firm, as we have pointed out, has stories to tell, if they have the will and facilities to seek them out. So identify the market for "softer", less news-oriented publicity. For example, every radio station has its own news magazine programme, usually following the early evening national and regional news on weekdays - but at other times as well. These programmes tend to be a mix of hard news, news features, offbeat items and local sport. They rely heavily on outside contacts to keep them informed.

Each programme will have a forward planning desk to map out future operations, and a news desk to shape the current day's output. If there are too many stories on the diary, a news decision has to be taken on which to cover. For that reason alone it is important to give the forward planning desk as

112

much notice as possible of your story/event, with the *guarantee* that it contains special or controversial ingredients which will give it an edge over the day's other stories, "hard" and "soft".

A further advantage with news magazine programmes is that you can establish yourself as the local expert in your given subject, so that you are called upon not only to comment on events happening in that area, but also to give local or regional reactions to national and even international stories.

The news/current affairs magazine programme deals largely, though not exclusively, in "human interest" material: perhaps "people stories" would be a better description. The accent is nearly always not purely on the nature of an event/planning decision/new factory, but on the impact it will have on local people. Quite rightly, the programmes regularly test public opinion on an issue through what are known in the trade as **"vox pop"** interviews (*Vox Populi* - the voice of the people). Microphones are taken into the street, and passers-by are trapped into speaking their minds - often with rewarding, even hilarious, results.

News magazine programmes will frequently feature sympathetic profiles of individuals battling against the odds, or they could have a bias towards arts-oriented "people stories", or use very often talented investigative journalists on local issues and controversies. They can then become targets for pressure groups who see them as ready-made platforms for their own particular views. There is every reason why you, your company or organisation should do the same. Get to know the presenters and producers of these programmes, put forward ideas which have local/regional appeal, especially if they are likely to be controversial or where the television or radio programme can claim to be championing a cause.

Programmes of this type - or, indeed, any current affairs programme, national or regional - can involve debates, and these sometimes turn out more like gladiatorial confrontations if sensitive issues are involved. If you are involved in this kind of discussion, it is a fatal weakness to sit back and wait to be called to speak. While you are saying nothing - or polishing the context of what you want to say - other, more aggressive, participants will jump in and steal your time. You must be similarly bold and aggressive. The single-issue fanatics will almost always rely on emotional appeal - while on your side you can offer only the truth, cast, regrettably, in the form of arid statistics or intellectual, unemotional argument. You will probably lose such an argument unless you adopt tactics similar to those of the opposition. And, of course, if the programme producer is getting good value from the opposition - "blood on the studio floor", metaphorically speaking - in a lively debate, then you may never be asked to speak, or at best, for only a short time. So make room for yourself: interrupt, but only at a point which will not annoy listeners. In fact you *must* interrupt if someone says something wrong or misleading. If you do not intervene to challenge a statement, the audience will assume that what has been said is correct. But even if you simply disagree with a viewpoint make your opposition known. The only qualification to this is if everyone starts speaking at once: when this happens - as it frequently does - no-one will be heard clearly, and the home audience will quickly lose interest.

It is also worth remembering that journalists and producers working in regional and local radio (and television) are likely to be highly ambitious: they may see their particular programme as the vehicle to national broadcasting. So never expect an appearance on one of these programmes to be easy: you could indeed find it a nerve-sapping experience.

The Studio Setting

Radio studios range from the awe-inspiring to the awful. An afternoon local radio talk-show host will sit in front of a huge console and has much to occupy his/her mind: talking, playing records and jingles, speaking to the people giving out the travel information, answering calls from listeners, twiddling a battery of knobs and buttons and somehow finding the time to ask you, the interviewee, a few searching questions.

Such people are hugely professional and the proof of this is that they make it all sound so relaxed when, in fact, it is a scene of constant, often conflicting, activity. What normally happens is that you are asked to present yourself at the studio 10-15 minutes before you are due on air. A researcher or programme assistant will normally greet you, or the presenter might pop out of the studio if a record is playing and he can get away. So make certain the producer/presenter knows precisely who you are, and why you are there. Do not allow for the possibility of a mistake: nothing will unnerve you more than to be introduced as someone else, talking about an entirely different subject!

Another type of studio setting which is possibly less intimidating, but is much more mysterious, is the studio where an interview is done "down the line" from a satellite station miles away. These "link" studios are sometimes primitive: you can be ushered into a room by yourself and told to get on with it. On the desk is a telephone, a set of "cans" (headphones), a microphone and a console box sporting an array of switches and buttons. On the wall facing you is a list of instructions. First of all, for example, you will have to bring the studio "on line" by pulling down the mains switch. After that the routine can, disconcertingly, vary from station to station, or region to region. One studio will involve a "forking key" to make contact with London; another a different button or switch. Cross your fingers and follow the instructions!

The Radio Interview

Chapter 6 deals in greater detail with interview techniques, but a few hints will help you feel more at ease.

When you are sitting comfortably at the studio table the first question you are asked will seem either innocuous or wildly irrelevant. It might be "What did you have for breakfast?" or "Did you find the studio easily enough?" (in an interview down the line). Relax: the studio is simply checking voice levels to make sure that you and the interviewer are speaking at the same level.

When the interview begins, remember that you cannot, on radio, contradict an incorrect statement or impression simply by shaking your head! You have to reply quickly with an authoritative "Nonsense!" or "That is simply not correct".

Although you will ideally be relaxed during the interview, a controlled charge of adrenalin is necessary to give your contribution an attacking edge: so try not to get too relaxed. Despite nerves, you must endeavour to come across as sincere and knowledgeable, but not overconfident and cocky. And bear in mind all the time that radio and television are above all entertainment: any performance should be as polished as a West End play. You must know your lines, and how to present them for the greatest dramatic effect.

Always be *positive*: say, for instance, "We are confident that we can win," rather than "There are lots of problems ahead, but we hope we can overcome them." Make bold, committed statements: "We will do..." as opposed to "We are thinking about..." Don't be discouraged if your performance falls a little short of perfection: almost everyone comes out of the studio certain that they they could have done better, or covered more ground, or made their points more forcefully.

It may sound obvious, but always listen carefully to the question: it is all too easy in a studio interview to latch on to a key word and get the wrong end of the stick so that you answer a question that hasn't, in fact, been asked. If you haven't heard the question properly, don't bluff the answer: apologise, and ask the interviewer to repeat it. In the same way, if the interviewer in his introduction or subsequent questions says something which is wrong, correct this before going on to answer the question. If the interview is being recorded, and you have made a mistake or left out a crucial point, ask for that question

115

to be put again, and supply the answer you want to appear in the interview.

Always remember that a seemingly innocent question might be designed to trap you into a damaging admission or statement. A favourite ploy is to begin a question with this sort of phrase: "I'm sure you would agree that..." or "Wouldn't you say that...?" Both are leading questions, and an attempt to put words into your mouth. If you say "Yes" because you lost track of the question and only agreed with the last few words, you are still on record as having endorsed the whole question.

Another point to watch: in a radio studio particularly, the presenter/ journalist has a great deal to do, and may appear not to be concentrating on your answer as he fiddles with a switch or selects the next jingle (if it is that kind of programme). Don't be led astray: they are professionals - and the next question will be fired at you as soon as you stop speaking.

Don't fall into a trap - or, even worse, trap yourself. If a question starts with the words: "Surely your product is just as dangerous as..." - be warned: this is a trap. The automatic response would normally be: "No of course it's not as dangerous ...", to which the journalist will then reply: "Maybe not *as* dangerous, but *still dangerous....*"

Do not tell lies: they will come back to haunt you; and once caught out, your credibility is in tatters. It is better to be honest - or, following the now time-honoured stratagem, "economical with the truth". If you do not know why something has happened, say so, but emphasise that everything that can be done is being done to find out what went wrong. You will come across as far more sincere and apologetic by answering in this way than by trying to wriggle out of responsibility or making excuses.

State the main points you wish to make in the way you have structured your interview. Never leave a propaganda point to "the next question": you may not be asked another question. If a big story breaks as you are speaking, you stand a good chance of being taken off the air to make way for a news flash. So state your case early in the interview - and, if you get the chance, repeat the main points to reinforce the message.

Try to personalise a subject: the programme will want you to do that, anyway. They have asked you to appear as much for your performance as for the knowledge you have. Tell the audience how a particular action or proposal will affect *you* - and, by extension, *them*.

Treat the interviewer as neutral: he/she almost always will be. If you are unlucky enough to be faced by a hostile interviewer - **and most people never will be** - you will just have to grin and bear it, and cope as well as you can. Remember, you will gain audience sympathy if the presenter - no matter how famous or well-liked - is seen to be too hard on, or unfair to, you.

Try to stick to the subject in hand, if you are allowed to, and avoid giving hostages to fortune by introducing material of a sensitive nature. Let the presenter do that: then you can always say something like "I am very sorry but this just isn't my area of expertise..." or "I really don't have any information on this."

If the interview has not gone well for you, it is still possible to turn the situation round by having the last word. Provided you know when the interview is likely to end, you may be able to hog the last few seconds to get a point firmly across. Generally, the last words listeners hear are those they remember, which is why throw-away remarks by a presenter at the end of an interview can be so devastating. It doesn't matter how good you were during the interview, or how cogently you put your case, if the interviewer's closing comment is "I don't believe a word of it", many listeners will agree with him. Professional broadcasters are adept at these oneliners and are experienced enough, should they choose, to turn almost any situation to their advantage.

In general, then, give fluent but precise answers of a reasonable length: avoid replying in monosyllables. If you answer questions with a one-word answer, you make it difficult to maintain the impetus of the interview. On the other hand, after you have said what you want to say, do not start groping around for more to say. That is not your responsibility: you are not there to fill programme space; that is the job of the presenter. So say what you have to say, and keep quiet. If you keep on talking, you will end up creating massive problems for yourself - including those avoidable "hostages to fortune". Answer questions as succinctly and persuasively as possible - then shut up and wait for the next question.

There are, of course, exceptions to recommended practice. Politicians, and other accomplished broadcasters, are past masters of the art of avoiding questions. There is, after all, no rule in broadcasting which says that you *have* to answer the question, and some politicians can go through an entire interview without addressing the subject matter. They see their job as putting across the message which they came to the studio to deliver. Besides, there are many ways of ducking a difficult line of questioning. Listen to the average political interview on a programme like "Today", and you will pick up some handy tips. For example, "That is a very interesting point, and I'll come back to it later, but first of all, let me say..." or "The question throws up lots of interesting ideas, but had you thought about...?" or "I'm glad you asked me that because it has reminded me of..." We could go on...

117

TELEVISION

Television is just as demanding as radio, although you have a visual presence to help you put across your point, whereas in radio the impact is made solely through the voice. But on television there is that extra requirement: you have to think not only about what you are saying, but also about what you are doing and how you look. The television camera can be cruel: it is pointless to select as a spokesperson anyone who looks incongruous on screen, however well they perform. Some people constantly move, blink or twitch when the camera is on them and this makes them appear shifty. Self-evidently, these do not impress as interviewees, because the viewer is likely to be distracted by what they are doing, rather than listen to what they are saying. To offer any distraction in a television interview can be fatal. There are others who are natural broadcasters who come across so well that they viewers instinctively trust and believe them.

The Studio

Television studios are daunting places - even satellite studios where interviewees face a remote-control camera, and possibly a monitor screen. It is a disconcerting experience. The interviewer could be hundreds of miles away, and you can feel terribly isolated if the sound link is lost, because you may not even know you are broadcasting. It is safer to assume that television cameras and microphones are always "live" - and behave accordingly. The television camera which is filming you actually has a small red light glowing at its apex, but treat it as though it were "live" all the time: it discourages you from bad habits like sniffing, snorting and (perish the thought) nose-picking.

Finding a television studio is often a major operation. Television sets are like film studios: a centre of light and controlled activity surrounded by a warren of dark passages and corridors strewn with a mass of cables. Make a point of arriving early so that you know the salient geography - programme office, hospitality room, make-up room and studio - and to talk to the interviewer. A researcher from the programme will have made the initial contact with you to get background and story material. You may not meet the presenter until you arrive at the television station, where you will be shown either into the programme office or into a hospitality suite waiting room.

The hospitality suites of big television companies usually have a selection of drinks, both alcoholic and soft, and comfortable chairs where you can sit and compose yourself before the interview, or unwind afterwards. Unwinding before the interview, cushioned by a large whisky, is a grave mistake.

118

Hospitality suites can be dangerous places. It is a golden rule never to drink alcohol before an interview - not even just one to steady your nerves: it is surprising how even one drink can affect your speech. Imagine you are appearing on the programme to extol the virtues of road safety, and speak with a distinctly slurred voice. You will certainly not win many converts, and are unlikely ever to be asked back.

Take a soft drink by all means - but refuse the offer (not always well-intentioned!) of spirits. You will not in any case want to drink much of anything: leaving the studio in search of a toilet midway through an interview will not win you many friends. It is while you are in the hospitality room that you make the first contact with the interviewer - unless, that is, the programme is already on the air.

Guard Your Tongue!

If you and the presenter do manage to meet for a general run-through of the core issues of the interview, be on your guard: give nothing away. The presenter will try to uncover juicy areas that he/she can then introduce into the interview. The slightest unguarded remark or reaction will provide the presenter with potent ammunition.

Always remember it is a journalist you are talking to: never say anything you do not want the media to know. With a really good story, and outside the conventions of an official briefing, there is no such cover as "off the record" or "this is purely background information". At the first sniff of an exclusive, such assurances go straight out of the window. So if the presenter asks probing questions about subjects you did not expect - nor were invited - to discuss, query the line of approach by all means...but don't answer them. Pregnant pauses can be used to great effect in these circumstances. The presenter who is on a fishing expedition will ask you, innocently enough, "There have been some dreadful stories about this company, haven't there?". He is hoping you will confirm the point and, believing the matter to be confidential, blurt out all sorts of indiscretions to back it up. Instead, you say nothing, or simply reply, "Really?" - and throw the topic back to the interviewer.

Nerves do play an important role in any television appearance. The thought of appearing in front of millions of people, of the need to "perform" well, and especially of how damaging it could be to do badly, can wreak havoc with your composure. Some people are so nervous before going on air, that they are in danger of saying something they wouldn't dream of saying elsewhere. This tendency must be avoided at all costs.

A managing director of a major company was invited to a regional television studio to talk about job propects in the area. During the pre-interview chat with the presenter, he was unwise enough to ask - "strictly off the record, of course" - for advice on dealing with what he termed "a rather sensitive media matter". The interviewer inquired what the problem was. The managing director explained that as part of a rationalisation plan, his company was likely to shut a factory in the area making about 300 workers redundant. What was the best way to handle this?

It was, of course, a classic misjudgment. Introducing the item the presenter said, " We are here today to talk about employment prospects in the region, but first we are going to concentrate on job losses. Joining me is Mr ————, whose company is shortly expected to announce hundreds of job losses in our biggest town..." The businessman was certainly ingenuous,

but unintentionally provided an invaluable object lesson: never volunteer information unless you have a very good reason to do so.

User-Unfriendly Places

Other problem areas associated with television and particularly with television studios, are (a) the blistering heat (for which few people are prepared) and (b) how telegenic you are. The heat of a studio when all the lights are on and focused upon you is a form of torture about which you can do virtually nothing, except to try to feel both relaxed and cool. It sometimes works; more often it doesn't.

The other problem might seem equally intractable - a television camera can be unbelievably cruel. It will sharpen the features of some people almost into a caricature, and to others apparently add pounds in weight. It has been estimated that the camera can make you look up to 7lbs heavier than your actual body weight, which is why so many television presenters seem to fight a continuing battle against a bulging waistline that in real life is scarcely noticeable. It is unrealistic to expect people to go on a crash diet for a television interview, so the best advice is that, provided you look reasonably ordinary, try to forget the camera and what it can do: sit up straight, and enjoy yourself.

Indeed, once you have done a few television interviews, and are more familiar with what is going on around you, you will be able to concentrate better on what you have to say, and on saying it in the most persuasive way. One tip is to blank out the thought that you are on television. Try to imagine you are sitting with a friend, discussing a subject about which you actually know quite a lot. That can get you in the right mood - although you should be wary of losing that edge of adrenalin that makes the crucial difference between a striking performance and a merely adequate one. Maintain eye contact with the interviewer, because you can pick up all sorts of signals from this, and by all means try to ignore everything else that is going on around you. This can be difficult: no matter how important you think you are, to the studio staff you are just another body being processed on the relentless treadmill that is television. Even while you are speaking, there will be people milling around, coming into and leaving the studio, making signals to each other, preparing the set for the next item, and so on. It is essential that you concentrate on what you are doing, and not on what is going on around you.

Never talk directly to the camera: nothing looks more like naked and unashamed propaganda (after the style of a party political broadcast) than a speech directed at the camera. Apart from anything else, a camera closeup of your face while you are talking will show every flicker of your eyes: if you appear distracted and look away, it could suggest to the viewer that either you are not comfortable with what you are saying, or are not really interested in being there at all. Shifting eyes imply a shifty persona.

Alone In The Lions' Den

A further disadvantage with television - and one which is impossible to overcome - is that interviewees tends to be isolated from what is going on around them. You may be sitting on a sofa or at a desk with your presenter, but he will have an ear-piece so that he can hear instructions from the control room up in the gallery - a place you will never even see. The floor manager and other studio personnel are also linked up to take directions from the producer in the control room. The only time you will ever be brought into the act is when the floor manager or presenter warns you that you will be going on air in, say, one minute. Otherwise, you an are unimportant cog in an intricate machine.

You might also get some indication of when the interview is drawing to a close. If you do pick this up, and you haven't already made your key points and by this stage you really should have done so then if nothing else, you know time is running out. It is up to you to monitor the progress of the interview - without darting surreptitious glances at your watch. But if the presenter feels inclined to help by saying "Finally...." or "If you could answer as briefly as possible...." that could be an invaluable hint that you have only 15 seconds or so left.

Finally, then, at the end of the interview, be it radio or television, (a) keep quiet, and (b) don't heave a huge sigh of relief until you know with absolute certainty that you are off the air, and that your microphones are dead. A studio is "live" until you have been told you can leave it. And even prime ministers and presidents can get caught out making unguarded comments to what they assume - quite wrongly - is a dead microphone!

One businessman recently spent almost ten minutes being interviewed about allegations that his finance company had been fleecing consumers by charging exorbitant commissions. His arguments were forthright and plausible, and listeners were left with the general impression that he and his company were the victims of a witch hunt, or at least that things were nowhere near as black as they had been painted. However, what would have been a superb interview ended catastrophically when, in the few vital seconds after the interview was concluded and the microphone was still live, the businessmen looked across the table at the presenter and was heard by millions to say: "If you believe that, you'll believe anything!". The only comment you should ever make in this twilight period might occur if the interviewer has concluded by getting in "last words" which are patently wrong or unfair. In that case, you can have the last word. The presenter may think the interview is over but that crucial period when the microphone is still on will give you the opportunity of saying something like "Rubbish", "Nonsense" or "Not true". And that is the viewpoint which stays with the listener.

As we suggest later in Chapter 6 on interview techniques, choose the live interview if it is offered, although there are advantages as well as disadvantages to an interview recorded either in a studio or on location. For one thing, if you make a mistake during a recorded interview, you can correct it by asking for the question to be repeated, and then answer it as you meant to. Indeed, if you are unhappy with the entire interview, they will almost certainly let you do it again, if they have the studio time. (They will always say they *don't* have the studio time: never let that put you off.)

The disadvantage of the recorded interview is that the journalist and his producer/editor decide the broadcast content: they can (and frequently do) leave out answers which you thought crucial. You have no control over what is screened, although you do have the right to complain if it is clearly inaccurate or defamatory. You are allowed the ultimate sanction of forbidding them to use the interview at all - but many television companies now ask you to sign a "release" giving them the right to edit and broadcast the material. The copyright belongs, of course, to them and not to you.

Live interviews are preferable **as long as you know what you are doing.** It is true that what you say cannot be edited out - but, by the same token, if you forget to make your key points, there is no second chance: unlike the recorded interview, they cannot be added later.

Appearance

Viewers may judge you as a first impression on your appearance and demeanour, before they start listening to what you have to say. It is advisable to go at least half way to meeting them by taking minimal precautions: comb your hair, and make sure your hands and nails are clean. You have lost the first battle if viewers' perceptions have already been influenced by what you are wearing, or how you are sitting, so the image you present is important. The clothes you wear for a television interview are very important.

Clothing, accessories and general appearance are covered below and in summary in Chapter 6, but one objective for which you should always strive is to be yourself. Never try to change your image into what you believe people think you ought to be like. Wear clothes that you feel comfortable in, because that will help relax you. They should be sensible, smart clothes that make you appear respectable and responsible, and which above all do not in any way distract the audience. Unless it is a very special occasion, don't rush out and buy an expensive suit of a type you would not normally wear. Instead, choose outfits you put on for special occasions, and take perhaps extra care - have the suit or dress cleaned, for example, and make sure your shoes are polished. On the other hand, if you are known for wearing casual clothes, stick with them. It hasn't done Richard Branson any harm, and a politician who is normally seen wearing a formal suit can come across in a totally different light if interviewed at the weekend in a cardigan or sweater.

As we have pointed out, a television studio can quickly feel like a furnace. You will be doing yourself a favour if you select materials that are less likely to make you feel hot or burst out in a sweat. Natural fabrics such as cotton are best, since many synthetic materials have a tendency to stick to you when you get clammy. Nylon and some other synthetics can also create static.

Pastel or neutral "soft" colours are best because they present you in a more comforting light.

Women should avoid flashy jewellery, which looks ostentatious and is also distracting. A charm bracelet will rattle every time you move your arm, and reflected light from earrings and necklaces annoys viewers. That is one reason why a string of pearls is so popular with many women who regularly appear on television. Strong colours - red, black, white - are sometimes too harsh. Wearing a black sweater against a dark background can make you "disappear", with only your head clearly visible. White plays havoc with clear definition. In the glare of the studio lights a bright white shirt tends to absorb you into the background.

Spectacles occasionally cause problems, especially if you have lenses that darken in strong sunlight. Leave them at home; if your eyesight is weak, try another pair of glasses. Viewers will find you both suspicious and distracting if you hide behind dark glasses. You should, of course, wear glasses if you need them: the lines of your face and expression will alter if you are peering myopically at the interviewer; but ensure that they are clean and dry before the interview begins so that they don't mist up in the heat. And check that alarms on digital watches are turned off -and, of course, leave your mobile phone well away from the studio. Finally, take a cotton handkerchief with you in case you need to mop your brow or blow your nose - but remember to put it out of sight after using it.

Don't be shy about make-up: it is essential for both men and women, and the lady who applies it is sensitive and skilful. The camera can accentuate harsh lines, and studio lamps will reflect off bald patches or shiny skin. In most cases, all that will be necessary is a little face powder, but an extended appearance might warrant the full treatment; and during a break in the interview, the make-up woman may come on to the set and give you another pat with her powder-puff.

Location Tactics

There could be an occasion when an interviewer or producer will try to persuade you to be filmed in a totally inappropriate setting, wearing gear in which you would normally not be seen dead. Put your foot down and refuse.

For instance, if you are being interviewed because your company has been accused of wasting millions of pounds in unnecessary expenditure, you will not wish to be filmed in the directors' leisure complex. Equally, if they want to film you in your office, choose somewhere which is going to show you in a favourable light: ie, hardworking and diligent.

Unless you are a business tycoon, you will not want to appear across a huge polished desk in a carpeted, oakpanelled office. The overriding impression that kind of setting gives is that you are "The Boss", and probably out of touch with your employees. Should the producer or cameraman suggests you wear something special as a "gimmick", say "No", because it will almost certainly be counter-productive.

Body Language

The wrong body language can send strong, antipathetic signals to viewers.

Television is a transient medium, so snap judgments are made on vital first impressions. The character assessment made of him/her by the viewer is formed in a few seconds: you like someone because they have a pleasant face - you don't like someone because they have long hair; that is the way prejudices operate. And that initial judgment will largely govern viewers' responses to the message of the interview. If they like the look of you, they are more inclined to agree with what you say - and, equally important, vice versa. It is extremely difficult to change that opinion no matter how irrationally it was formed.

Assuming you have taken that first hurdle, your subsequent body language - fertile territory for psychologists and psychiatrists in recent years - is also going to weigh heavily with the audience. How you sit, your facial expressions, eye movements, hand gestures and so on, can all signal messages to the interviewer and audience in a way that words cannot. Use those gestures that make the most impact: shaking your head when you disagree with something is very effective on television. You don't even have to say anything: if you are on camera, viewers know immediately how you feel. And if the camera isn't on you at that particular moment, it soon will be when you shake your head so demonstrably and emphatically.

Margaret Thatcher used to employ a single gesture so imperious that it instantly gained control of the situation. She would forcefully hold her right arm out with the palm of her hand towards the speaker. It was such a powerful "stop" signal that discussion invariably came to a halt, and she was instantly able to regain control of the situation. Lady Thatcher knew (and still knows) full well the dramatic impact the gesture would have, which is why she used it. Television is, by its very nature, a dramatic medium, and modest gestures will largely go unnoticed. Registering disagreement with a small shake of the head is not enough: you don't have to bang the table, but a response somewhere between is necessary if you are going to put across convincingly how you feel to both the viewer and the interviewer.

Eye contact is a significant aid for conveying sincerity: eye bonding creates control, which will pass to the presenter if you cannot meet his/her gaze. Experienced waiters are particularly adept at this. That first eye contact can determine who is going to be in charge the waiter or the diner and some waiters deliberately set out to pre-empt the situation by establishing their superiority with looks, gestures and comments made as you place your order. It has to be said that most waiters, certainly the best ones, do not adopt this attitude, but the example illustrates how important it is to establish the rules of engagement at the first meeting.

The programme presenter's objective is - or should be - to inform and entertain his audience through his guest. Interviewers quickly lose audience sympathy if they demolish a guest, or constantly try to score points - unless it is a politician. They can be considered fair game, and most people enjoy the spectacle of politicians suffering a hard time, especially if they refuse to answer questions directly. Don't waste sympathy on politicians: they can look after themselves.

Having established the eye line, maintain it if you can. Should you find absolute eyeball-to-eyeball contact disconcerting, pick a spot just to the left or right of the interviewer, but at eye level so that the camera will capture you as if you are looking directly at him.

Furthermore, by studying the eyes of the interviewer you can gauge whether he is excited by your answer, confused by it, agreeing with you, becoming angry, and so on. All this information helps you to adjust your own approach: depending on the signals you receive, you can appear more challenging, or more conciliatory, and perhaps take greater care to explain yourself. The eye line is necessary when you are asked a question: losing it might indicate a lack of interest. It is discouraging for an interviewer if the guest is staring into space or looking at his hands folded in his lap. And look naturally at the interviewer: don't glare or stare, because the viewer will immediately register this as aggressive or menacing. Try not to let your gaze wander. It is distracting for viewers to see your eyes darting all over the place, clearly demonstrating that you are not concentrating.

Expert analysis of eye contact has thrown up a few ground rules that are worth remembering:

- **Always break contact by looking down. Turning your eyes upwards might indicate impatience, whereas by looking down you are signalling thoughtfulnes, humility and non-aggression.**
- **Flickering glances to left and right suggest shiftiness - even though the probable reason is that someone has distracted you by walking into the studio.**
- **If you are distracted and this is reflected in eye movement, it will also confuse the viewer, who will study less what you are saying than what you are doing.**

Smiling occasionally - not fixedly, and not permanently - will convince viewers that you are genuine and human, and have a sense of humour. However, there is an entire gamut of smiles. The "knowing" smile relays the message: "I knew you were going to ask me that, and I have a complete answer..." There is the "sympathetic smile which means: "I really do

126

understand your problem...." There are degress of smiling - a slight grin can be as effective as an ear-to-ear smile. So don't overdo it, and practise your options in the bathroom mirror to assess the different emotions and reactions you are arousing.

Hand and arm "language" is a powerful indicator of feeling: a clenched fist clearly expresses antagonism/jubilation, just as an outstretched hand is a welcoming or friendly gesture. However, in a television interview you should attempt to keep your arms and hands under control - though use them, by all means, if you normally do, but limit your gestures to keep within camera frame. Be careful not to cover your mouth with your hand: it creates a barrier between you and the viewer, it will probably muffle your words, and it signals strongly that you are either nervous or have something to hide. Another common habit is rubbing the side of your nose. Studies suggest that this particular nervous tic produces soothing sensations which can calm people down in times of stress. Certainly, being interviewed can be stressful, but resist the temptation. It will convey to the presenter and the viewer that you are not in control of the situation, otherwise you wouldn't be doing it!

Sitting with your arms firmly crossed also denotes a barrier between you and the interviewer, according to pyschologists, either because you have something to conceal, or simply because you are afraid. If you are nervous, clasping your hands in front of you can stop them shaking. Don't twiddle your thumbs or do anything else that might distract.

There have been many studies into what people unconsciously do with their hands. Some touch the side of their mouth over and over again, others play with their ear-lobes or pat their hair into place. Most of these gestures have become such a part of our personae that we don't even know we are making them - but during a television interview you have to concentrate on controlling them. In the same way, some people repeatedly lick their lips when they are nervous - a guaranteed instant turn-off for the viewer.

A well-known broadcaster developed an infuriating habit of jingling coins in his trouser pocket while he was speaking, asking questions and listening to answers. It became so distracting that interviewees were unable to concentrate. Eventually, his producer was driven to have him searched and stripped of all loose coins, keys and other tinkling items, confiscating them until after the show. In fact, that is a good precept to follow: remove any such items from your own pockets before you go into the studio in case, like the unfortunate broadcaster, you may have absolutely no idea that you are jingling.

Crossing your legs can prevent you from nervously tapping your feet, but if you are already tense you might suffer an attack of cramp or pins and needles, so that when you try to stand up you have a dead leg and topple over! Women feel more comfortable with their legs crossed at the ankle, but should remember to keep their knees together. Leaning back and away from the interviewer implies that you are trying to distance yourself from him, whereas if you lean slightly towards him you are being attentive as well as signalling that you are trying to close the gap between you.

Whether or not you believe the psychology of body language, the interviewer will watch you as closely as he/she listens to you. Your posture and behaviour tells the presenter a great deal about how you are feeling - and thus how to handle the interview. So opt for a comfortable, sensible sitting posture.

During one of our television training sessions with a group of senior executives, we actually lost one of them down the back of the settee. The executive was trying to give the impression of being totally relaxed, so he lounged rather than sat on the settee. As the interview progressed, he started to sink down between the deep cushions and the back of the settee until only his head and shoulders and ankles and feet were visible. It took two people to haul him from the depths of the settee, and the interview, while hugely comical, did not get across any of the right messages. That is why in every sense it pays to keep both feet firmly planted on the ground.

The Television Interview

You will be afforded every chance to say whatever you want to say during the interview: indeed, you are there *because* you have something to say. Unless you are a controversial figure, the idea behind the interview is not to embarrass, expose or injure you, or even to probe difficult or sensitive areas (although if they emerge they *will* be probed). The programme's objective in almost all cases is merely to question you on matters you know about; provided you do know the answers, you should have nothing to fear.

Seasoned and polished broadcasters may give the impression that they have an enormous command of most subjects: in reality they do not. Most interviewers will have developed a high level of general knowledge, but unless you are appearing on a specialist programme with specialist presenters, then you, without any shadow of doubt, will know more about your subject than the programme presenter. After all, the reason why they want to interview you in the first place is because **you are the expert**.

The interviewer will have done some of his own research, or the programme staff will provide him with a list of questions from which to select, or to act as a guide for framing his own. This research will be drawn from a variety of sources. First of all, the interview has to be topical, so some mention of the topic is likely to have appeared in the papers in the last day or so. Failing that, the information may have come from your company in its own annual report. If the source is the former, then what appears in the newspaper will largely dictate the type of questions that are asked; therefore, if there were any inaccuracies in the article, they will be reproduced in the programme - and must be corrected by you.

Few people nowadays will subscribe to the once common belief that everything they read in the papers is true. Perhaps newspapermen constitute the sole remaining section of the population that does *still* believe that. At any rate, the fiction is reinforced by newspaper and agency libraries who keep cuttings, from their own and other sources, on all major events, personalities, companies etc. Each day, the library staff will look through the newspapers and cut out pieces which they think may be useful later. When a story breaks about the company or person in a few months' time, the reporter draws the relevant file from his library to read up the background. The trouble comes when a newspaper cutting is inaccurate and the correction (in the unlikely event that one was ever printed) is not included in the file. The reporter assumes the file is accurate - but the resulting story, based on it, may contain a number of major errors.

When your television interviewer flourishes those same inaccuracies, you have to correct them, because if you don't challenge the mistakes, the audience will assume that what has been said is right. You should naturally try to do this in a way which does not reflect on the interviewer. First of all you want to avoid alienating him/her - and secondly, regular presenters of radio and television programmes have both long memories and armies of fans, who will side with them, against you, if you appear too critical.

Media Training

Media training courses usually for a maximum of six participants - are designed to prepare people for appearing as an interviewee on radio and television. The aim is not to transform someone overnight into an accomplished broadcaster, but to place participants in interview situations and instruct them in basic - and more sophisticated - broadcasting and interview techniques. At Mediawise Communications we brief candidates on how to spot traps set to catch the unwary, and give instruction in dealing with awkward subjects and controversial points.

As part of the course, participants are interviewed on two main subjects.

One is notified in advance, so they have time to prepare ideas and responses in the way we have outlined in this book. The other is on a subject given to them with no prior notice, which normally proves our recommendation that all interviews, however short, must be structured in advance: there is a strategy for every subject and every occasion.

We believe we can demonstrate how important it is to be able to deal confidently and convincingly with broadcasting journalists to gain maximum impact for your message, and optimum benefit to your company/organisation's image.

Below is a brief summary of the Mediawise approach to interviews:

Research

By definition, a news interview will always be at short notice -but try to secure enough time for adequate research. Ask for specific information on:

- the subject
- the degree of detail required
- the type of programme and audience
- the duration of the interview
- the content of at least the first question.

Preparation

You are the expert in an interview, but there are still a few basic rules to observe:

- learn your brief
- master the key elements of your subject in concise, "bullet point" form
- isolate three essential points you wish to make
- make them
- choose your words carefully
- avoid jargon, technical and bureaucratic
- speak colloquial, graphic language
- use terminology everyone can understand
- be precise, but emphatic.

Points To Note In The Studio

1. Discuss the elements of the broadcast with the interviewer. You won't want to be caught out by questions that lie outside your current knowledge.

2. Speak in your normal voice, but project it because you have an important

message to convey. If you have a regional accent, do not attempt to disguise it.

3. Try to ignore the microphone: speak to the interviewer all the time.

4. Be alert and in command your confidence will be heard.

5. Speak clearly and distinctly. Remember that on the radio the listener cannot see you the audience can judge you only on how you sound.

6. If you need notes, make them brief preferably on a card and clearly written or typed, laid out ready to read. Don't shuffle pieces of paper.

7. Assemble the facts to avoid long pauses.

8. Be sincere, committed and enthusiastic. That is the only way to interest your listeners.

9. Use your voice as a weapon: it is the only one you have. Vary pitch, speed and timbre without extremes. But don't gabble.

10. Listen to accomplished radio performers (like Alistair Cooke) to identify their strong points.

11. Monitor the progress of the interview.

12. Don't be sidetracked, or weighed down by extraneous material.

13. Refute incorrect statements.

14. Don't be too defensive.

15. Try to anticipate surprises.

16. Don't use the interviewer's first name it smacks of collusion.

17. It is, in any case, the listener whom you are addressing.

18. Try not to say "Well..." or "I think..." at the start of every answer.

19. Don't fill embarassing silences that's the interviewer's job.

20. Only hesitate if it is a deliberate pause.

21. Don't lose your temper.

22. Don't volunteer irrelevant information.

Mediawise Communications
Oakhurst
Crown Gardens
Fleet
Hampshire GU13 9PD.
Telephone : 0252 622301.

Chapter 6

INTERVIEWS:
TACTICS AND TECHNIQUES

This chapter deals with the tactics and techniques of media interviews, reinforcing some of the points made in the previous chapter. The section is followed by interview scenarios (national and local) and analysis.

Tactics

Defined below are a few basic points about appearing on radio and television, and suggestions on the correct way and the wrong way to respond to an interview in a critical situation. The advice is illustrated by a number of plausible scenarios, with, towards the end, contrasting versions of the same brief interview.

Whether it is on radio or television, the approach to the interview itself is identical:

- prepare *thoroughly*
- isolate three or four main points to make
- devise the best way of stating your case in a **conversational** style that suits *you*
- but avoid jargon and pomposity, complicated constructions, unfamiliar initials or acronyms, and confusing statistics
- don't make lists of points: they never work
- aim always for clarity
- use precise, trenchant, but colloquial language
- structure the interview properly for maximum impact
- no answer should exceed 30 seconds!
- you are looking for:
  - a strong, committed opening
  - a way of gaining, and holding, audience interest
  - a positive, up-beat conclusion
- formularise your replies

- commit them to memory
- you must sound both knowledgeable and sincere
- rehearse your performance at home or in the office
- double-check the timing in rehearsal.

Basic Practice

Whatever its subject matter, an interview is still a *conversation*. Even though you are addressing possibly millions of people, you are still *talking* to just one person. So don't let this lead to confusion in your mind: speak to the interviewer, rather than try to go over his/her head to the invisible audience beyond. Where you are communicating with that audience is in what you say and the way you say it; but your remarks must be directed at the programme presenter.

Any "gear change" from the conversational to the pontifical mode will grate horrendously on the listener - and especially on the viewer. An interviewee who breaks the eyeline contact in a live television interview to face the camera directly is no longer taking part in an interview: he is making the equivalent of a party political broadcast.

Always use your natural voice: if you have a regional accent, you need not exaggerate it, but don't attempt to conceal it. If you are speaking in what is, for you, an affected or mannered voice - for example, in Southern Standard English when you normally talk in identifiable Yorkshire/Somerset/Suffolk "dialect" - you run the risk of sounding at best artificial, and at worst ridiculous.

You will be talking at approximately broadcasting speed: three words a second. If you keep to this pace, you will remain intelligible at all times. But do not feel inhibited from breaking that rhythm, for the sake of emphasis and impact.

Remember that on radio, the voice is the sole weapon at your disposal. It is only by subtle changes in timbre, pitch and pace that you can convey particular commitment or conviction. If you feel passionately about the subject of the interview, then demonstrate that feeling in what you say and the way you say it. As long as you avoid sounding hysterical, you will not forfeit audience sympathy. They are accustomed to the bland: a little fire can be a welcome relief.

Say What You Mean: Mean What You Say

Being committed implies an undeviating endorsement of the cause which you represent; being positive lends even greater force to that commitment.

133

So faced with an argument or proposition with which you profoundly disagree, make that disagreement both obvious and absolute. To such a challenge, you can safely reply, "That's simply not true"; or "That's nonsense"; or, more devastatingly, "Rubbish". You need add nothing more by way of imprecation: it will alienate the interviewer if you go on to suggest that he/she is being misguided or, worse, naive, in asking that particular question. Simply limit the process of destruction to the one, straightforward, denial, and then state the reason, which would normally be encompassed in one of the three or four key propaganda points which you were, in any event, going to make.

An apparently small point, but one which can, nonetheless, create an unfortunate impression, lies in the use of first names between you and the interviewer. A general rule to follow is that you should try never to use the interviewer's first name, even though you, and the audience, know it well enough from daily acquaintance. In the minds of some listeners or viewers, it can suggest an unacceptable degree of collusion between yourself and "Jeremy", "Brian", "Trevor", "Martyn" or "Jim", carrying with it the presumption that you are old friends who have somehow worked out the interview between you in a way which makes both of you look good. On the other hand, to persist with "Mr Paxman", "Mr Redhead", et al., will seem not just pedantic, but positively priggish. And, needless to say, to call Jimmy Young anything but "Jimmy" makes you, not him, look silly. It is, therefore, better not to employ any form of address at all. Keep it neutral: the message, not the person, is the important constituent of the interview.

Make It Work For You

At the forefront of your mind, at every stage of the interview, must be the central thesis that you are engaged in a propaganda exercise. You are there not to impress the audience with the exotic flavour of your personality, but to win approval for your cause. Indeed, a bizarre personality can be counterproductive: like a heliotrope bow tie or a vicious squint, it can detract from the impact of the message. If viewers, or listeners, are studying you, then they are clearly not listening to what you are saying. If it is your misfortune - televisually speaking - to look like the Princess of Wales or Robert Redford, then you have lost the argument through no fault of your own. People at home will be saying, "Doesn't he look like Robert Redford?" - and the first minute of your interview will have sunk without trace. **But**...if the power of your delivery and the substance of the message are convincing enough, you may still win them back.

134

So concentrate all the time on delivering that message. To a degree, you can even ignore the precise content of the question put to you. Don't forget that your interview task is to make the three or four propaganda points which you have previously identified, laboriously structured and painstakingly learned. If you get a question which takes you well away from your main platform, you will simply fend it off in the ways we suggested earlier. So don't be sidetracked: make those points you came there to make. Say only what you want to say; above all, never offer information which has not been sought.

However, you will obviously try at all times to be as helpful as you can to assist the presenter in shaping a rewarding interview. So avoid at all costs monosyllabic answers. It may strike you as clever to limit your reply to a laconic "Yes" or "No", but a moment's serious consideration ought to convince you that this tactic will confuse and even infuriate the interviewer, and will not impress the audience. In a three-minute interview, allowing a minute to the presenter for his introductory cue and the questions he puts to you, the time allotted to you for the answers which constitute the gravamen of your propaganda case is around two minutes.

Do you really want to waste perhaps 15 seconds of your precious time in giving a supercilious reply which can only result in the presenter repeating his question and demanding that you make a proper response? That is not the way to make effective propaganda. Next to the value of the propaganda you have been given the opportunity to make, the quality of the interview should be a prime consideration for both you and the programme presenter. After all, if you are seen to do well, you are likely to be asked back. And if you enter the filing system, you might end up joining the programme's repertory team of reliable interviewees. There are worse fates!

From the programme's/station's viewpoint, then, the ideal interview will be one that is at least newsy, and at best controversial. It must end on time (morning television and radio programmes, in particular, have a number of "opt-out" points which they have to meet), and contain no awkward silences which the presenter has to paper over. If it leads on to further audience participation (by phone-in or follow-up), all well and good; if it gets newspaper (especially national newspaper) publicity for the programme, that is a considerable bonus - for which the programme will be duly grateful to you.

From your point of view, the ideal interview is one that was properly structured at the preparation stage, and ended on the right "feel-good" note after you have made all three of your strong propaganda points with maximum impact. If you come out of the studio thinking, "I wish I'd said *that*" then you have only yourself to blame. But nobody is saying it is easy...

INTERVIEW SCENARIOS

National:

The following fictitious scenarios demonstrate interview techniques for enlisting audience sympathy rather than hostility in nationally or locally critical situations. They are not necessarily intended to stand as the definitively "right" or "wrong" way to do the interview.

News has emerged through a local stringer of an outbreak of cholera in a popular resort on the Greek holiday island of Crete. There are 40 dead - including one British child - and the epidemic is spreading; hospitals are filling up. It is the height of the season. Jackson's Holidays have 650 package tourists scattered among five hotels in the town which is the centre of the epidemic - Agios Nikolaos - and a further 2,400 throughout Crete. IRN has contacted Jackson's Public Relations Officer (PRO) in London.

INTERVIEWER: You've heard what's happening on Crete: what are Jackson's doing about it?

PRO: Let me say first of all how very concerned we are at this cholera outbreak, and the danger it represents to our holidaymakers. We're desperately sorry that there have already been fatalities, and we hope the epidemic's now been confined. What we're doing straight away is not to add to the problem by sending even more people to Crete: we've cancelled all flights to the island from last night onwards.

INTERVIEWER: Cancelled them indefinitely?

PRO: Of course. People who've booked with us will get a total refund, and we'll advise them when it's safe to go there again in case they can rearrange their holidays. We're also liaising with other major holiday companies through ABTA - that's the Association of British Travel Agents - to try to arrange a joint action programme. Nobody's in competition on something like this, so let's work together for the safety of our customers.

INTERVIEWER: What about looking after the people who are already there?

PRO: A medical team is already on a scheduled flight to Crete. They're travelling with top Jackson's executives, who'll arrange for every single British holidaymaker on the island to be medically checked and inoculated against cholera. If any of them already have the disease, we'll place them in local hospitals and fly out their relatives on scheduled or special charter flights. If anyone's worried enough to want to cut short their holidays and come home immediately, we'll arrange that, too.

INTERVIEWER: At your expense?

PRO: Naturally. We don't think about money at a time like this. What matters to us is the safety and comfort of our holidaymakers. That's our sole concern - and our reputation in that department is very high indeed.

Analysis: The public relations officer gets full marks for expressing concern and sympathy at the very outset. She then goes on to make her three propaganda points in logical answers to direct questions: holiday flights cancelled with full refunds; a medical team on its way to inoculate everyone; free flights for relatives of sufferers and Britons wanting to come home early.

****

Another holiday peak season story. There has been a series of charter plane incidents - aborted take-offs or landings, flight diversions owing to mechanical failures, etc - and two actual crashes (one British), all affecting old aircraft of a particular make...call it the Rocket 811. Like other firms, Pioneer Airways (a charter airline) uses old Rocket 811s. Overnight there has been a third crash in New Zealand. Pioneer Airways' chief executive is in the radio car for the "Today" programme.

INTERVIEWER: I know none of your planes has been involved in these incidents, but there are Rocket 811s in your fleet, aren't there?

CHIEF EXEC: There are indeed - and, as you say, they're performing well. But these accidents - and particularly the crashes - are terrible, for airlines and travel firms as well as for the poor people on board. I'd like to express our deepest sympathy to the relatives of all the deceased, from wherever they came.

INTERVIEWER: I'm sure that will be appreciated...but what precisely are you going to do about these Rocket 811s which are still flying the Pioneer flag?

CHIEF EXEC: I can tell you now, on this programme, that as of today we

137

are withdrawing every one of our Rocket 811s from service. They'll be thoroughly examined and overhauled. It may not be necessary, because they are regularly checked and serviced pre-flight anyway, but we cannot, we dare not, take chances with the lives of our passengers.

INTERVIEWER: So what are tourists who've already booked with you going to fly abroad in?

CHIEF EXEC: They needn't worry. No-one's going to lose their holidays, because we're already in the process of replacing our Rocket fleet with newer aircraft. Let me emphasise that we don't have to do this...We don't need to. I have every confidence in the Rocket 811s used by Pioneer Airways - but, if there's the slightest doubt about their reliability or performance -

INTERVIEWER: Which there clearly is...

CHIEF EXEC: Yes, of course there is! I'm not denying that. The doubt exists...therefore, as I see it, we have no alternative but to remove that doubt by withdrawing the aircraft from service. But that doesn't mean to say that we believe those particular 'planes to be dangerous. If we had thought they were, we wouldn't have kept them in the air.

INTERVIEWER: So you'll be sending holidaymakers out today, and from now on, in newer chartered aircraft. But what about the people already on holiday who're due to fly back home in Rocket 811s?

CHIEF EXEC: The same will apply to them. We'll either switch them to scheduled flights, with Pioneer making up the differences in fares, or we'll get the new chartered 'planes to their airport of embarkation in good time for the return trip.

INTERVIEWER: An expensive business.

CHIEF EXEC: Not where people's lives are possibly at stake.

INTERVIEWER: And indeed have been lost...You've defended retaining these 811s in your fleet - even though you're now taking them out of service. But you could easily slip them back into use when all the fuss has died down. Should you really be trusting people's lives to 20-year-old 'planes?

CHIEF EXEC: I think you've made your point. I doubt very much if we'll recall these particular aircraft...though I must insist that they are not, in the opinion of our expert engineers, dangerous. The aircraft - all the aircraft - in our fleet are subjected to the most minute and rigorous tests and examinations before they're declared airworthy. I would ask you to believe that we do not take chances with passengers' safety.

138

Analysis: Again, the right priorities: sympathy first (doubly effective since Pioneer are not involved), followed by the three propaganda points: Rockets withdrawn; Rockets replaced; people already abroad brought home in alternative aircraft. Clearly the withdrawal of the Rocket 811s would anyway have been forced on this company and others: Pioneer has pre-empted this, and turned the withdrawal to its advantage - while at the same time giving the programme a first-class news story which would have gone out on the Press Association wire as a "snap" almost as soon as the words were spoken. It is a good example of damage limitation, and of gaining credit from adversity.

****

This scenario is based on a real-life incident. There has been a fire at a luxury hotel in a Mediterranean country; 17 people died, including a British journalist, one of a group of travel writers staying on a "freebie" under public relations control. Breakfast television have brought the hotel public relations officer up on a satellite link.

INTERVIEWER: I realise you must still be in deep shock, but have you been able to find anything out about how the fire started?

HOTEL PRO: We are all in shock...horrified at the terrible loss of life...that this should happen at an Oceania hotel, with our reputation for safety is...well, almost unbelievable. Our hearts go out to the bereaved. They are in our thoughts and prayers.

INTERVIEWER: And the cause of the fire?

HOTEL PRO: In so far as I am able to, I'll come on to that shortly. But I would like to emphasise the total commitment of all the hotels in the Oceania chain to the safety of our guests. I can tell you now that the management has ordered a comprehensive review of all safety procedures to try to find out what happened - and what, if anything, went wrong. We are obviously cooperating wholeheartedly with the local police and fire authorities.

INTERVIEWER: So - a safety review. But are you still open for business?

HOTEL PRO: Obviously not. You can see the damage for yourselves. We're making arrangements to transfer all the other 800 guests to other hotels at our expense, so that they can complete their holidays in comfort. Anyone who has lost possessions will be immediately, and fully, compensated by the insurance cover which we provide for them as a normal practice.

INTERVIEWER: I'm sorry to have to press you again - but do you have any idea how fire could have broken out in a building which, according to you, is as safe as Fort Knox. It shouldn't have happened, should it?

HOTEL PRO: It's really much too -

INTERVIEWER: And when it did happen, guests surely ought not to have died if your safety procedures are as good as you say?

HOTEL PRO: I'll try to answer the question, if you'll allow me to. The fire only happened last night. It is far too early to say with any assurance how it started, or even where it broke out, and how it spread so quickly so that people were trapped on one of the upper floors. That investigation is a matter for the fire authorities and the police, not for Oceania Hotels. One thing I can tell you at this stage is that repair work has already started. It should take no more than a week, so there need be no interruption to anybody's future holiday plans.

Analysis: As with the first two scenarios, she got the priorities right: sympathy and shock; comprehensive safety review and helping to find out what happened; transferring guests to equivalent hotels, and repairs within seven days. Here the exercise in damage limitation is itself limited: the damage to the hotel is tangible; people have died. Her aim was to calm the situation down, stress the group's safety record, and prevent the hysterical transference of possible danger to other Oceania hotels. As a footnote, what happened in real life was that the hotel spokesperson uttered no expression of sympathy for the dead and bereaved, and made no form of commitment to improve safety standards. Astonishingly, she is even on record as saying that "in a fire on this scale, 17 deaths out of 800 guests is a reasonable score". As experts noted at the time, the interview simply added a public relations disaster to a human tragedy.

****

People have found ground glass in three different kinds of Drinkwater's renowned pickles and chutneys, bought at supermarkets in the north-east of England. The evidence is in the hands of the police, who are investigating whether the contamination was accidental or intentional. So far, only 11 incidents have been reported, involving powdered glass or splinters. In each case the adulteration was detected immediately, and there are no casualties. A local radio station, quick off the mark, has found Drinkwater's Technical Director.

INTERVIEWER: How did this glass get into your products?

TECH DIR: It really is impossible for me to say at this stage. At the moment, that's a matter for the police. We're tremendously upset here that it's happened, and very relieved indeed that no-one's been hurt. And I'd like to apologise to any of our customers who've suffered anxiety or inconvenience over this matter.

INTERVIEWER: But you're Drinkwater's Technical Director: you must know your company's procedures. How could a thing like this occur - unless somebody did it deliberately?

TECH DIR: You're jumping the gun. If you're implying someone is trying to blackmail us, then it's news to me.

INTERVIEWER: There's been no approach...phone call...letter...that you know of?

TECH DIR: None. And if there had been, I would be telling the police about it, not your listeners.

INTERVIEWER: Are these pickles still on the supermarket shelves - being bought even now, as we speak?

TECH DIR: We've done all we can. We've faxed all supermarkets and grocery shops throughout the north-east with an urgent warning to their customers. The next step will be to withdraw the products. I am confident that can be managed today - but it's a big logistical exercise. We're following up our faxes with visits to as many supermarkets as we possibly can, and we're also contacting the people who bought the contaminated jars.

INTERVIEWER: Do you think the trouble might be a fault in your production process?

TECH DIR: As I've told you, the circumstances are being investigated by the police, and we are helping them in every way we can. Beyond that statement I cannot, and will not, go.

Analysis: This is tricky territory. The product contamination is small, but the recall is hugely expensive, and the very act could constitute an admission of liability. However, the public would be satisfied with nothing less than recall. Although Drinkwater's reputation will inevitably suffer, delay might lead to a fatality, and an expensive law suit. The Technical Director probably ought never to have agreed to the interview in the first place, but the outcome is not a total disaster. He should not,

though, have introduced himself the possibility of blackmail, nor have volunteered the information that there had been no blackmail approach, when he could not be absolutely certain about this. Better tactics for the company would have been to muzzle its executives and refer all inquiries to the police, after making a simple statement to the Press Association about the recall of the product.

****

Five sixth form pupils - three boys and two girls - at a renowned co-educational public school have been expelled. The school is well-known as a centre of liberal education, with the older pupils encouraged to take responsibility for their own behaviour. The expellees - one the daughter of a marquess - were discovered participating in a sex "orgy"; amphetamines and other drugs were found in their possession. More seriously, a junior girl, aged 15, was with them, and reported indecent assaults on her that stopped just short of rape. The Independent Schools Information Service and its media consultants have coached the Headmaster into his first television interview since the story broke.

INTERVIEWER: Headmaster - sex orgies, drugs, a very serious offence against an under-age girl...your school doesn't come very well out of this, does it?

HEADMASTER: I disagree. This immensely regrettable incident doesn't reflect either on the school's reputation or on the quality of education we give at Selway House. The responsibility belongs where it has been assigned - to the pupils concerned. They behaved in a foul and reprehensible way, and we have dealt with them. Selway House will recover from this tragedy...for the future of education in this country, Selway House must recover.

INTERVIEWER: The school is famous - you could almost say notorious - for its, shall we say, explicit approach to sex education - even for children below the age of sexual consent. Do you not think that this sort of freedom and licence invites behaviour of the sort we have here?

HEADMASTER: No. If I believed that I would amend the style and nature of the curriculum. We do not teach our pupils to fornicate and take drugs.

INTERVIEWER: You teach them to "explore sexual contact", as I understand one of your staff puts it?

HEADMASTER: We teach them to inquire into, and be aware of, the nature of homosexual and heterosexual love. That is a very different thing.

142

INTERVIEWER: Is it? Were these sexually-active sixth formers simply "inquiring into the nature of love" when both sexes committed disgusting acts with the younger girl?

HEADMASTER: What they did was unforgivable. It had nothing to do with love, and everything to do with perverted lust. If their...attitudes and...actions were at all the result of encouragement they imagine they had received from the form of sex education practised here, then I am deeply sorry that this should have happened. But they were grossly wrong: what we try to teach is tolerance and humanity.

INTERVIEWER: Tolerance, yes...you're tolerant of pupils caught smoking cannabis, I believe.

HEADMASTER: If by that you mean we do not expel them, that is correct. It has happened five times in ten years - and on each occasion the offence was not repeated.

INTERVIEWER: This incident happened in daylight, in the school grounds, Headmaster. What sort of protection can your staff claim to give to young, vulnerable children, if a group of drug addicts and fornicators - to use your word - is allowed to behave in this fashion?

HEADMASTER: To say that any pupils at my school are "allowed" to behave like these did is a distortion of the facts, and -

INTERVIEWER: But they did do these things. And nobody stopped them!

HEADMASTER: They were discovered, and they were dealt with. Look - you must understand...there has been no other remotely comparable incident in the history of Selway House. To answer your question: yes, we do offer our pupils protection - but we cannot protect against the entirely unforeseen. I can assure the parents of every child at Selway House that the staff are constantly vigilant in supervising the safety and well-being of the children. But there was no indication that these particular sixth formers were indulging in loathsome practices of this type.

INTERVIEWER: Yet they...

HEADMASTER: The overwhelmingly important consideration is, first, that the young girl who was the victim of these acts should recover, in mind and body. And then that this...appalling incident...must not be permitted to...destroy...or even to harm... a school which is unique of its kind, and offers an education of unparalleled breadth and achievement. It is done with! It will not happen again. Please...let us get on with what we do best.

Analysis: The Headmaster will have earned the admiration of his peer group and, to a degree, limited the damage done to his school. But he will not have impressed "ordinary" people (who know little of the ethos and traditions of an institution like Selway House) with his elitist arrogance. To them, the issue is black and white: the orgy, the drugs, the violation of the girl -these are acts familiar to them, because they happen in the night-time streets of their own neighbourhoods, where the offenders - the unemployed, the abused, the dregs of society -end up in jail. But in this case the perpetrators are privileged, wealthy and free. Although Selway House parents may be won round, the public - especially the tabloid media - will not forget.

****

A sharp freelance journalist in the north-west has filed a story that a number of people from one small village have been taken ill - with two hospitalised - after drinking apparently contaminated tap water. The newly privatised water undertaking believes the supply to this isolated area has become adulterated after a chemicals mix-up at their purification plant. They want to be sure of their facts before they admit what might turn out to be an expensive liability. They would prefer to say nothing at this very early stage, but rather than condemn the company with a potentially damaging "no comment", their resources planning director agrees to meet a crew from the regional television station in the village concerned.

INTERVIEWER: How do you think your water supply has become contaminated?

RES DIR: Who says it is? Nobody knows yet. That might turn out to be the case, and certainly the people affected have, so I'm told, reported drinking straight from the supply, but we simply don't know what has hit them in this way.

INTERVIEWER: They seem to think it was the water. That's what they told us, anyway.

RES DIR: Look...I'm as sorry as I'm sure you are that people have been taken ill, and particularly distressed that two of them are in hospital. As soon as we received notification of this, I immediately ordered a full-scale investigation to try to trace if the water supply is responsible. That investigation has hardly begun. Until they report to me - and, incidentally, to the public health authorities, with whom we're working closely -until that happens, I simply cannot speculate about the cause. One thing I will say: if the water supply to this area is contaminated, why haven't more people been affected?

INTERVIEWER: That may be happening. Besides, the sick are all old people.

RES DIR: So I believe - and they, and the very young, are the most vulnerable. Let's hope no-one else will be affected...as they won't if they do as we tell them.

INTERVIEWER: Which is?

RES DIR: That just in case - and I stress the "in case" - the supply has become adulterated, people must not use their tap water for consumption in any way; and indeed, avoid using it at all if they can help it.

INTERVIEWER: That's a tall order! Can't they just boil it?

RES DIR: If it's a bacteriological adulteration, then boiling the water would protect them. But it would have no effect on, say, an accidental chemical contamination.

INTERVIEWER: What are they to drink, then - and what are you doing to help them?

RES DIR: If you look over your shoulder - and if the camera can follow you - you'll see for yourself what we're doing. That large vehicle just entering the village is a water tanker. It'll be joined by five others within the next hour. The water they'll carry has tested out as completely pure. I hope that within the next few moments there'll be a long queue at that tanker. And I promise the people of Little Gidney that they won't go thirsty tonight.

Analysis: Good tactics, these: no admission of liability or assumption of responsibility; concealment of what the company knows to be the cause, while preparing the ground by putting chemicals in the frame; an announcement of a public investigation; strong advice to consumers; and - a real bonus of the location interview - immediate and practical help for people in a desperate situation. As it is, the film of the water tanker cruising down the village street, together with a sound bite from the resources director, not only leads the regional bulletin, but makes the national news as well.

****

It is Budget Day, and a teetotal Chancellor of the Exchequer is expected to impose an increase in both duty and VAT on imported wine. One of the programmes covering the Chancellor's speech live takes the precaution of bringing in a wine company executive to join an already crowded panel of experts. Somewhat smugly, the Chancellor makes the anticipated announcement - emphasising that English-grown wine will not be affected, and that if Britons choose to buy expensive and unnecessary foreign drinks, they must be prepared to pay a premium for their self-indulgence.

PROGRAMME PRESENTER: Well, there it is, Don Philpott: ten per cent on wine duty plus an increase of no less than five per cent in VAT? Fair, would you say?

PHILPOTT: It's grossly, spectacularly unfair, of course. Wine is a pathetically easy target for the Chancellor - who admits he doesn't even like it. It's imported, so the traffic is easy to regulate and tax; it's regarded by unsophisticated people like the Chancellor of the Exchequer as an unnecessary, even sinful, luxury; and because it's a largely foreign product, the Government seems to think that making wine more expensive is something that won't damage the home economy.

PRESENTER: Which you obviously feel is not going to be the case?

PHILPOTT: Definitely not. In this country, wine is by no means a luxury tipple for the rich. Many millions of ordinary people drink it, and see it as an entirely necessary accompaniment to good food. These people don't deal in bulk with smart City wine merchants: they buy their wine a few bottles at a time from their local off-licence or supermarket. If High Street wine sales plummet, then the off-licence chains are going to shed staff. That doesn't appear to matter to this Government.

PRESENTER: So - possible unemployment. What about consumers - they can buy more English wine, presumably?

PHILPOTT: They can, and I hope they will. But I have to point out that home-grown wine not only lacks the variety of wine from the traditional climates, it's also more expensive than the best medium-range French or even Australian vintages. So this is without doubt a bad deal for consumers.

PRESENTER: The Chancellor must think it makes sense, though, otherwise he wouldn't be doing it, would he?

PHILPOTT: He must indeed, though why I can't think. The immediate effect of these increases will be that people will buy less wine. They'll stick to their favourite foreign brands rather than sample the dearer English

146

product, but they'll get one bottle instead of two, half a case rather than a whole case. Therefore the Government will end up receiving less duty from the dearer product than they got before when it was cheaper. If I didn't know our revered Chancellor was teetotal, I'd be tempted to think he was the worse for drink when he dreamed this one up!

Analysis: In the right hands - and Mr Philpott is an accomplished performer - this interview is a gift. He selects culpable targets: the Government and its non-drinking Chancellor. He reduces the argument to a populist level: wine is drunk by ordinary people, not just the rich; if sales fall, jobs will be lost; in the end it will mean less, not more, money in the Government's coffers. The Chancellor tries conspicuously in his speech to play the patriotic card ("We are a nation of beer drinkers": "English wine will not be affected"). Mr Philpott turns this argument against the Chancellor by the simple expedient of ignoring it, and ends with a joke at the Chancellor's expense.

****

Magnet Garden Machinery gets reasonable publicity from a Silly Season launch of a campaign to find the country's perfect "small house" lawn - ie, one looked after by the householder rather than by a company of gardeners. And of course, the owner must already use a Magnet lawn-mower. Three days into the campaign, a 12-year-old boy living in the Home Counties is killed in an accident involving a Magnet lawn-mower in his parents' garden. The campaign has rebounded on Magnet with a vengeance. There is no point in the company trying to avoid publicity, since three days earlier they were actively seeking it. The "perfect lawn" campaign was the idea of Magnet's thrusting young Sales Director. It is only fitting, the management decides, that he's the one who should be thrown to the wolves.

INTERVIEWER: Well, your campaign has certainly made the newspapers!

SALES DIR: Oh, come on, this is the sort of publicity nobody wants. A boy is dead, using one of our machines. It's a human tragedy, and we feel desperately sorry for his family and friends. For a young life to be wasted in this...senseless way is sad beyond description. I would ask you to believe, though, that this was a horrifying *freak* accident. It should never happen again. It ought never to have happened at all.

INTERVIEWER: And it might not have happened if you hadn't offered a first prize of £50,000 for the so-called perfect lawn. It was a big incentive to a lad like Paul.

SALES DIR: Lads like Paul should never have been allowed near his father's lawn-mower. Magnet lawn-mowers are not toys - and they're not for children.

INTERVIEWER: According to his mother, he was all fired up by the competition. And the lawn was his, wasn't it? He normally cut it.

SALES DIR: With a small, hand-pushed machine and an edging tool, so I was told. That's a far cry from a much heavier self-propelled machine which simply ran away from him until he fell into it. Unfortunately, it happened on a day when his father was at work, and his mother had popped next door for a cup of tea with her neighbour.

INTERVIEWER: You don't, then, accept any responsibility for trying to increase your sales by putting up a prize big enough to "fire up" a boy like Paul? We'd all like that kind of money, after all.

SALES DIR: None whatsoever. My conscience is clear. The prize is not disproportionate to the effort required for the standard of lawn we have in mind, and there was no way we could anticipate such an event. I repeat - properly handled, our machines are safe. They are not, however, constructed to be chased across a lawn by children. As I said: it was an appalling, but freakish, accident. As for the "perfect lawn" campaign, we shall continue with it, and hope that this terrible incident will serve to persuade parents everywhere that children must be kept away from machines which they cannot control.

Analysis: On the whole, the Sales Director did not do too badly. He was assisted by a misguidedly "flip" opening from the interviewer, and stated his case well. The important ingredients certainly are: it was a freak accident; the machines, correctly used by adults, are safe. Here, the Sales Director uses a highly recommendable strategem: if your defence is based upon one or two crucial points, then structure the interview to start and finish with those points. If you have nothing else to say, or are simply trying to defend the indefensible, repetition can be extremely effective.

****

A Scottish landowner has bought 5,000 acres of the north-west High-lands, which he intends to seed with fir tree plantations. There have been press stories about wealthy people using plantation tracts in the Scottish "Flow Country" as tax-beneficial investments. The landowner is a professional forester, but the acquisition is unusually large. Also part of his new land is an officially designated Area of Outstanding Natural Beauty, and some of his trees, when they are grown, will straddle a hill overlooking a beautiful loch, and completely spoil the view. Various countryside organisations have tried to contest both the deal and the afforestation plan - but both are perfectly legal, and there would seem to be no grounds on which a successful objection could be lodged. The landowner, Mr McMurtrie, agrees to appear on "Newsnight" down the line from Glasgow. The interview follows some very pretty film of the area which, it is alleged, he is bent upon despoiling.

INTERVIEWER: You've seen that film, then, Mr McMurtrie. Surely you must agree that the countryside is extremely beautiful, and that it will not be improved by your planting about a million fir trees there.

MCMURTRIE: I didn't need the pictures to tell me how lovely my country is, thank you. I know the land well. As to the second part of your remarks, I will not be simply dumping a million fir trees, as you call them, haphazardly on the ground. I shall plant in well-designed and properly managed conifer plantations, to produce something which Scotland and the rest of the United Kingdom badly needs: timber, grown on a sustainable basis.

INTERVIEWER: To make paper, I suppose.

MCMURTRIE: Some of it, yes. The point you don't seem to be taking in is that it costs Britain literally billions of pounds a year to import all the wood we need. We grow barely more than 12 or 13 per cent of our annual requirements. I'm trying to save taxpayers like you and me a lot of money. And I'm not destroying a great natural forest to do it, either. I'm growing my own.

INTERVIEWER: But in a place which surely to goodness doesn't need unending plantations of conifers marching across a landscape which is naturally desolate...rolling hills, gentle dales. Such a profusion of trees is unnatural in that sort of countryside, is it not?

MCMURTRIE: I don't accept that. A million years ago it was probably covered with trees. It's been shaped by agriculture and erosion. I'm bringing the trees back.

INTERVIEWER: Against the wishes of practically every conservation or environmental group in your country, Scotland.

MCMURTRIE: And might they not seem, to people in this city of Glasgow, or your city of London, to be massively selfish and bigoted people? What, after all, are they saying? "Don't touch this land, because I want it to stay as it is so that I can sit and look at it. Don't plant conifers here because I don't approve of conifers". No-one dares to criticise these fashionable fanatics or do anything of which they disapprove. Yet it doesn't matter a fig to organisations like these what people in London, or in the rest of Scotland, want. Their only concern is what *they* want. It matters to **me**, though. I want to bring industry and jobs to this fallow land. I want to create wealth, in a natural and sustainable way. I want to make Scotland profitable and productive. For Scotland's sake, the countryside must **live**. It must not be allowed to fossilise, preserved in amber for the selfish ends of a few hundred envious town-dwellers with no roots in the land. Listen to the **people**. They **live** there!

Analysis: One may not approve of Mr McMurtrie, but he marshals his arguments and presents his case with real fire and passion. In some ways, it is an object lesson in how to stand up to pressure groups, who are not always as selflessly altruistic as they pretend to be. Unfortunately for McMurtrie's case, the last word - either on that programme or on the following evening -would probably have gone to the environmental pressure groups on the grounds that they speak for neutral but concerned people. McMurtrie takes a calculated chance that the power of his rhetoric will gain him public sympathy which ought to have gone to his opponents. If he does win the first battle, it is more by courage and luck than by judgment. And he will almost certainly go on to lose the war.

INTERVIEW SCENARIOS

Local

Here is a set of equally valid (and equally fictitious) "local" interest scenarios treated in a different way, in contrasting pairs of interviews. Interview "A" is, in each case, either aggressive or mendacious, or simply incompetent; Interview "B" is a fairer statement of the case, and more likely to gain audience sympathy. They are set as they would be on regional television, either studio or location.

150

This is based on a local authority plan for a major road widening scheme in the centre of a town in the television station's franchise area. The plan will lead to closing off part of the town's High Street for six months. The item has been illustrated with film of the roadworks and shoppers negotiating the High Street obstacle course, plus an interview with the district council planning officer. The tailpiece is an interview with a front line shopkeeper, Mr Brown.

Interview "A"

REPORTER: Could you give us your reaction to this plan, Mr Brown?

BROWN: It's scandalous! Simple as that! They might as well come round to my place tomorrow morning and shut it down for good. It'll kill the High Street for passing trade - and we rely heavily on passing trade.

REPORTER: But you've got local customers as well. Surely they'll be happier, and safer, shopping in a traffic-free High Street.

BROWN: They might - if there were any shops left to go to. I can give you the names of seven, including my own, that'll be forced into bankruptcy by this scheme. What's the use in widening the street if you're going to destroy local traders?

Analysis: Mr Brown has a valid point, but he is clearly motivated entirely by self-interest, and almost ruins his case by overstatement. Interview "B" is a more sympathetic way of getting his message across.

Interview "B"

REPORTER: Could you give us your reaction to this plan, Mr Brown?

BROWN: It'll be fine when it's finished, but how are old people, young mothers with prams, the disabled...how are they going to cope with a torn-up road? It's a death-trap. And that's entirely apart from the effect it'll have on our businesses.

REPORTER: What do you mean?

BROWN: I seriously doubt whether many High Street shops, including my own, could survive a six-month traffic closure of the High Street. We rely heavily on passing trade.

REPORTER: But local customers ought to enjoy a traffic-free High Street, surely?

BROWN: Yes - if they can get down it without breaking their necks!

Analysis: Brown now starts his defence not with the effect the road closure will have on his business, but rather the distress it will cause vulnerable groups. He introduces the question of his lost trade almost as an afterthought. In the first interview he is blustering and self-centred; in Interview "B" reasonable and conciliatory. That is the vein in which he and his fellow shopkeepers will be shown to the best advantage.

****

Another High Street shopkeeper saga. This time, a greengrocer, Mr Black, has been criticised by passers-by, and warned by the council, for leaving out refuse which attract scavenging animals, who then spread it across the street. It's not a big story for the regional news programme, but it has public health overtones, and the station has some decent film of the High Street littered with rotten vegetables and fruit. They round the piece off with a two-way with Mr Black outside his shop.

Interview "A"

REPORTER: Well, you've seen those pictures, Mr Black. That's your produce, left outside your shop, that the neighbourhood's cats and dogs have dragged all over the main shopping street. What have you got to say about these criticisms?

BLACK: What does the council have to say, you mean, don't you? I've told them time and time again that I've got perishable refuse that needs collecting every night, not just once a week. They've done nothing about it - nothing. It's not my fault, it's theirs. What do we pay council charges for...tell me that!

REPORTER: You surely can't expect the sanitary department to collect from you six days a week, while everyone else has to make do with one day?

BLACK: Why not? They're the ones who're complaining. I've only got one place to dump it - and I can't keep it inside my shop for six days.

Analysis: Mr Black obviously has a predicament, but presents it badly, and counter-productively in terms of council co-operation and public sympathy. He blames the council and accepts no personal responsibility. He expresses no remorse at the nuisance he's caused, and will have made no friends with this petulant outburst. There is a better, and much more effective, way of putting his case.

152

Interview "B"

REPORTER: Well, there's the evidence on film, Mr Black. What are you going to do about it?

BLACK: First of all, let me say how truly sorry I am if I've been causing a public nuisance and given offence to anyone. But I do have a real problem. I can't keep this rotten produce in my shop for a whole week; and I can't dump it at the back of my shop, because that's someone else's garden. What choice do I have?

REPORTER: Couldn't the council make an emergency collection for you if, as you say, it's a public nuisance?

BLACK: I've asked them. The answer's no. I bag the stuff up as tightly as I can, but still the dogs tear it apart. Stray dogs, of course. I want to help, but I'm just about at my wits' end. I'm afraid it's up to the council sanitation department now. Short of eating the stuff up myself I've gone about as far as I can go.

Analysis: The contrast is obvious. Black now gains audience sympathy by stating his apology first of all, and setting his problem in that friendlier context. He even refuses to blame local owners' dogs, preferring to lay the trouble at the door of "strays". And he still makes it clear that the Council must try a little harder to help in what the public will see as an exceptional case. He even ends with a little joke!

****

A bigger story now.

The major employer in the television region's principal town is planning to make a lot of staff redundant. As companies do, they have tried to keep the plan under wraps...but, of course, it has leaked to a local freelancer, who has alerted the regional newsroom. When the firm's public affairs department finds itself under siege, the managing director, Mr Foster, decides that he, and he alone, is capable of putting the right gloss on a serious situation. He offers himself for a live studio interview, which follows library film, interviews with off-shift workers, and their families on a local estate, and a heavily critical piece by a trade union regional official.

Interview "A"

REPORTER: Let me put to you the straightforward question, Mr Foster. Are you going to lose a thousand jobs in Norwich?

FOSTER: What we have in mind - and it is only, at the moment, in the planning stage - is a sensible rationalisation programme. And, incidentally, it would have been far better for everyone concerned - for Ephemeral Industries and its workforce - if we'd been able to announce this - this - rationalisation in our own time.

REPORTER: And no doubt in your own way - with a thousand redundancy notices. But it still comes down to that, doesn't it? You're going to throw 1,000 men and women on the scrap-heap.

FOSTER: It comes down to a gross interference with business practice by people like you. These things can be managed if they're done - eh - properly.

REPORTER: Mr Foster, you cannot expect to keep something like this secret from the people who've worked for you for many years and made you a very rich man. Now: are you going to sack a thousand people?

FOSTER: We have to cut costs! We rely to a vast extent on exports - and, in case you hadn't noticed, there's still a recession in most of Europe and our other markets further afield. If we aren't to cut corners on a world-renowned product - and I absolutely refuse to do that - then we must trim our costs. We're a labour-intensive company, so the savings we must make will have to be in the workforce...but I must emphasise that no irrevocable decision has yet been taken.

REPORTER: I'm sure your staff will be relieved to learn that, Mr Foster.

FOSTER: They will realise, as I do, that there is simply no alternative. We trade in the real world - and it's tough.

Analysis: This interview is only slightly exaggerated. Foster handles it about as wrongly as it could be handled. The fact is that Ephemeral Industries has been "found out", and although Mr Foster refuses to answer direct questions (because his Public Affairs Director has told him not to), he is actually telling the truth. However, he has succeeded in forfeiting any sympathy for his firm, and understanding of his case. To begin with, he might just as well own up to the planned redundancies - even though he would have preferred to make the announcement through a coded message in the Financial Times.

Interview "B"

REPORTER: Let me put to you the straightforward question, Mr Foster. Are you going to lose a thousand jobs in Norwich?

FOSTER: Yes, we are. I was planning to make the announcement tomorrow, but however you put it, that's the bottom line.

REPORTER: So why are you doing it?

FOSTER: God knows we don't want to. Some of these men and women have been with us for 30 years and longer. They're not just my employees...they're my friends.

REPORTER: Why sack them, then? You haven't answered the question.

FOSTER: Why redundancies? Well, as you probably know, we rely hugely on our export trade. And as you also know, exporting is a great deal more difficult than it was only a few years ago. The reason for that is quite simple: the worldwide recession.

REPORTER: But it's a quarter of your workforce you're getting rid of, isn't it?

FOSTER: Yes, because we're no longer profitable. We daren't cut corners with our products: that might put people's lives at risk. So we have to cut our costs. There isn't any real choice. Let me put it to you this way...if we didn't take this step we're now contemplating - and no final decisions have been made; I must stress that - but if we didn't at least plan to rationalise by about a thousand jobs, then sooner or later, as night follows day, we'd be driven into insolvency...and that would destroy another 3,000 jobs.

Analysis: This time, Mr Foster comes clean, and the result is a shorter, tighter and much more friendly interview. He also makes the point that he is not remote from his staff: the people who must go are his friends. He is then allowed to make his case properly, in an atmosphere free of rancour, and although the result - 1,000 redundancies - will be the same, the Managing Director has bought time, gained understanding of his company's insuperable problems and, quite possibly, made friends.

****

A regional/local news story frequently develops from a national source: from Whitehall, directly from Parliament, or from the Common Market...that sort of thing. The regional television newsrooms task is then to localise the story. In this scenario, a national survey has attacked the standard of car servicing at garages. The station has sent a crew to the forecourt of the biggest garage chain in their area. The boss, Mr Long, is not one to mince his words.

Interview "A"

LONG: It's rubbish! Everything they say is rubbish! We wouldn't be in business five minutes if we behaved like the cowboys they've turned up!

REPORTER: You admit there are cowboys, then?

LONG: So the report says. I've never met any as bad as these. I haven't read it through, but I reckon this survey's homed in on every whingeing motorist who's ever written to the Automobile Association, and then scoured the back streets of London and Birmingham for evidence. I run a business. I can't afford to treat my customers like that.

REPORTER: Like what?

LONG: Like some of these scare stories in the newspaper, that's what. I've never come across a garage that services cars like some of these bozos in the report.

REPORTER: You can seriously claim you've never heard of shoddy workmanship, neglect, or sheer ignorance on the part of servicing mechanics?

LONG: There's a tiny minority, perhaps...but not at Long's Motors. Ask my customers. Ask them!

REPORTER: Well, actually, Mr Long, we have asked them...

Analysis: Mr Long carefully digs the trap for himself, then falls straight into it. As it is perfectly entitled to do, the station planted a camera crew round the corner from Long's Motors service reception bay, and doorstepped a few customers. Some were less than flattering about the standard of servicing. Long, of course, has not actually read the report, and only skimmed newspaper versions of it. He is so used to fending off criticism of garages that he has developed what he considers to be an impregnable approach: attack! On this occasion, his interview is followed in the regional news slot by those with his dissatisfied customers - who steal the show. It need not have happened that way.

Interview "B"

LONG: Yes, I'd be worried if I thought this kind of practice was at all widespread. Though I must say that, having read the report thoroughly, it does seem to me that some of the cases cited are pretty extreme.

REPORTER: No cowboys, Mr Long?

LONG: Oh, they exist - but not, I believe, on a large scale. The industry is aware of these problems, though, and respectable garages go to enormous lengths to try to make sure it doesn't happen in the way the survey describes.

REPORTER: Nothing like that at your own garage, then?

LONG: That's where you're wrong. I'm aware there have been servicing complaints from customers of Long's Motors. The difference between us and the cowboys in the report is that I did something about it straight away!

Analysis: In this happier version of the interview, Mr Long's more conciliatory and fair-minded tone lets him off the hook. When he admits to justified complaints about servicing at his own garage, the programme decides not to run the customer interviews.

****

Not all news is bad news - but through sheer incompetence, even good news can be turned into something approaching bad news. For example, it is a red letter day in the life of local employer Standard Widgets plc when they are given the Queen's Award for Industry in recognition of their superb export performance. Standard Widgets plc do not believe in wasting money on media training. Their chief executive, Mr Robinson, a pillar of the Rotary Club, is supremely confident in his own eloquence. For a man who can hold his own with the best of them at the Red Lion every Tuesday lunchtime, a mere gogglebox interview is pretty tame fare.

Interview "A"

REPORTER: It's probably an unkind thought, Mr Robinson, but some people might feel you got this award because you can't sell enough Standard Widgets on the home market.

ROBINSON: That's right! Uh...I mean...that's right, it is an unkind thought. After all, we achieved high sales levels in the United Kingdom before we started sending widgets to Africa.

REPORTER: Do they need widgets in Africa, Mr Robinson? More, say, than they need food?

ROBINSON: Uh...I suppose they must. They buy them, anyway.

REPORTER: In large numbers, evidently. So you get a Queen's Award for selling expensive widgets to a country whose people may not need them?

ROBINSON: Expensive? Well, it's a top quality article - and that means top prices.

Again, a trifle exaggerated, perhaps. But Mr Robinson has virtually thrown away a priceless publicity opportunity -priceless in the sense that you cannot buy air time of the sort that is here given you for nothing. Or if you did have to pay for it, then it would cost you an enormous sum of money. Fortunately, Mr Robinson isn't really that sort of chap at all. He is grateful for the chance to appear on television in a non-controversial setting, and profited from media training - given him by a fellow Rotarian - to work on the interview and polish his performance. Interview "A" was a bad dream in the small hours of the night before the big day. Here's what really happened.

Interview "B"

REPORTER: It's probably an unkind thought, Mr Robinson, but some people might feel you got this award because you couldn't sell enough Standard Widgets on the home market.

ROBINSON: They'd be wrong. We reached maximum penetration - in fact, saturation - here in the United Kingdom, and that's what prompted us to look overseas. Our research showed us that Africa was wide open for our products.

REPORTER: Do they need widgets in Africa, then, Mr Robinson? More, say, than they need food?

ROBINSON: Of course not - but there again, I don't regard malnutrition in Africa as a fitting subject for a joke. But on reflection...yes, they do need Standard Widgets in Africa, in the sense that the whole world needs them. And believe me, with 25 per cent of our production now going for export, we've only just begun.

REPORTER: Exporting's expensive these days, though, isn't it?

ROBINSON: Not for people who've done their sums right. To survive in the export market, you've got to be competitive. And we are very competitive.

Analysis: Mr Robinson gets to the heart of it this time: a swift dismissal of the opening probe, a sharp put-down (permissible in the circumstances) on the question of the famine in Africa, and a sensible plug for his company in winning what is, after all, meant to be an extremely prestigious award.

****

For our final local example, we turn to sports sponsorship. Any company should be able to reap credit from supporting one of its local sporting organisations. The players or athletes, their supporters, the community at large...they all benefit from such a superficially altruistic act - perhaps not so altruistic, since the sponsoring firm also, of course, enhances its public profile. In the television interview when the announcement is made by Mr Jones, Chairman of the Biggleswick Building Society, all the cards are on the sponsor's side. It is simply a matter of presentation. The society employs specialist media consultants -but, naturally, Mr Jones doesn't need their help.

Interview "A"

REPORTER: This is breaking new ground, Mr Jones - a building society sponsoring a minor league football team.

JONES: It might not appear to - um - flatter our - um -traditional...image, I suppose you might say - um - traditional image of responsibility and - well - gravitas, as it were, but...um...we must move with the times, mustn't we?

REPORTER: If that's all you're trying to do, it might argue that you don't especially want to support a fairly unsuccessful team like Biggleswick United. Is that so?

JONES: Well, of course we do - otherwise we wouldn't be giving them all this money - although, since you mention it, they are a little way down the league table, aren't they?

REPORTER: One from the bottom, actually.

JONES: Oh...

REPORTER: Might it not be just a question of trying to get publicity for the building society, Mr Jones? You know...name in the programme, on the hoardings at the ground? And, of course, a seat in the directors' box for you and Mrs Jones.

JONES: Really? Uh - what I mean is...good heavens, no! We're -uh - ploughing back profits into the community. We're not asking for any credit for what we're doing.

REPORTER: In that case, you could have made an anonymous donation. Couldn't you, Mr Jones? Mr Jones?

Analysis: Mr Jones could scarcely create a worse impression. His opening is pompous, stilted and hesitant, and by mentioning "moving with the times" he actually feeds the interviewer with the material which sets the unfortunate tone for the rest of the interview. He reveals

ignorance of the team and its performance and, finally and disastrously, paves the way for a devastating onslaught on his and his company's motives and credit. Had he talked the projected interview through with his media consultant, the result would have been something more like this.

Interview "B"

REPORTER: This is breaking new ground, Mr Jones - a building society sponsoring a minor league football team?

JONES: Like Biggleswick United, our building society is very much part of this community. We want to give something back to the people we serve. And if you're implying that sponsoring football doesn't chime with the traditional image of the building society...well, all I can say is that the image is probably too stuffy, anyway.

REPORTER: Unkind people might suggest you were merely trying to get publicity for the society, Mr Jones. You know...name in the programme, and on the advertising hoardings...a seat in the directors' box?

JONES: And if they were really unkind, might they not also wonder why a patently successful building society should wish to ally itself to a pretty unsuccessful football team. Luckily, that doesn't concern us...and neither will seeing our name in the programme cause us to break open a magnum of champagne. No -we're not doing it for what we can get out of it. I know Biggleswick United aren't likely to win the Cup - or even stay in their own division. But if our support can help restore pride in the team and success in their game...that's the only reward we're interested in. If it's good for Biggleswick, it's good for the society.

REPORTER: Very commendable, Mr Jones, but -

JONES: One final thing, if you'll forgive my interrupting you. That seat in the directors' box - I don't need it. I've already got a season ticket for the stand, and I use it at every home match.

Analysis: Little more need be said: Mr Jones clearly wins on penalties by a fistful of goals. He puts the image question well, discloses a casually thorough knowledge of the team's prowess, and ends with a strike which would not disgrace Gazza!

Chapter 7

HANDLING A MEDIA CRISIS

This chapter tells you how to handle a media crisis, covering contingency planning and crisis action.

Strategic Planning

It is pointless to say, "It will not happen to us". You never know when a crisis will arise. It could happen tomorrow. You must be prepared.

Crisis planning is neither difficult nor expensive to implement: the advantages far outweigh any minor inconveniences. Bad publicity in the event of a crisis could destroy your company and credibility. With the right sort of advance preparation you will know how to react - and that provides the breathing space needed in order to pull through.

If not managed successfully, any delicate or threatening situation can develop into a crisis. But a crisis can be controlled - or even averted - if it has been anticipated, and provided everyone knows what to do as soon as it arises.

Therefore, as an integral part of media planning you must action this hit-list:

- identify risk areas and develop appropriate contingency plans
- establish an effective crisis control team with clearly defined areas of responsibility
- devise triggers for actioning contingency plans
- appoint spokespeople trained to deal with the media
- prepare position statements/media responses for all eventualities
- circulate an "Action Guide" setting out all the above-mentioned points
- regularly review and update/revise the guide.

161

Identifying At-Risk Areas

These areas can be divided into four categories:

- internal matters which could have serious operating consequences
- external matters affecting the organisation and trade/consumers
- external matters affecting the organisation and the media
- external third party problems which might impinge on your organisation.

Internal Matters: might concern the sudden departure of key directors, loss of vital computer data, a serious financial crisis, problems with suppliers, or any potentially embarrassing disclosures.

External Matters: affecting trade/consumers could include food terrorism, contamination faults, foreign bodies in products, complaints about deliveries, pricing structures, quality, need for product recall and so on.

External Matters: affecting the organisation and the media would arise when, for example, a wine company is plagued by scare stories, true or otherwise, about illegal substances found in products, widespread consumer/ Environmental Health Officer/trading standards complaints, or attacks by the specialist press over wine quality/prices.

External Matters: involving third parties could concern, say, a trade union faced with complaints about unions in general, their links with the Labour Party, activities of socialist governments overseas, or the damaging affects of another union's strike. These complaints/media attacks need not be directed specifically at your union, but they could nonetheless yield damaging spin-offs.

Every aspect of your company/organisation's activities has to be studied to identify potential risk areas. Plans to be amalgamated into the "Action Guide" can then be drawn up. Risk areas can include:

- In-house crises: over-reliance on key personnel, a major fire, loss of computer data, product contamination (deliberate or accidental), the use of illegal substances (or, in the case of wine, inferior corks), and product recall of any type.
- Manufacturing/distribution problems: strikes, delays, wrong labelling, poor storage, involvement by innuendo (malicious campaigns), media/trade attacks, damaging publicity on a consumer programme.

162

- Health issues: drink/driving, food and diet, environmental pollution.

At-risk areas can be identified only by management and key personnel studying their own spheres of responsibility and determining weak links in the production, packaging, distribution and marketing chain. Short thinktank sessions will home in on potential problem areas, which can then either be remedied or taken into account as part of the Action Guide. These sessions must be held at regular intervals to evaluate and reasssess risk areas, and appropriate responses to them.

The Crisis: Be Honest And Efficient

The media response to any crisis should follow the same pattern:
- muster the crisis team as speedily as possible
- identify the facts
- implement the Action Guide to contain the situation
- meet afterwards to debrief and assess the effectiveness of the Action Guide.

Contingency plans for all eventualities should be rehearsed as "dry runs", and ideally at short notice, to try to recreate the urgency that must be felt when the team goes "live". Rehearsals can also identify shortfalls and omissions in planning and lead to improvements.

The Crisis Team

You need:
- a co-ordinator to oversee the team, and monitor and evaluate activities
- a chief media spokesperson, with backup help as required
- a trade (and other interested parties) liaison officer, ideally someone with production and marketing knowledge
- external consultants
- support staff
- a logistics officer responsible for ensuring that:
  □ vital equipment is regularly serviced and working
  □ there are plentiful supplies of paper, fax rolls and computer discs
  □ there is a comprehensive logging system of the whereabouts of key personnel, arranging "on call" rotas.

163

The support staff will include:
- switchboard/clerical help
- people able to operate computers, word processors, fax machines and photocopiers
- volunteers to run messages and provide catering.

External requirements:
- access to legal, financial and insurance representatives
- round-the-clock messenger/bike services
- 24-hour access to press release distribution agencies
- telephone engineers for rapid installation of extra lines.

The crisis team must be thoroughly versed in its brief and be available to swing into action immediately a critical situation develops. The handling of the crisis in the first few minutes and hours will largely determine success or failure.

The team will work to the plan recorded in the Action Guide, yet still retain the flexibility to act as needs determine in rapidly changing circumstances.

Never rely on one person to handle the crisis: he/she may have gone on leave the day before to a remote island without telephones!

CRISIS ACTION PROGRAMME

The aim of all crisis management is to contain the incident as speedily as possible by identifying the cause of the problem and resolving it; by limiting the impact; and by implementing a communications strategy which keeps key external parties informed - strictly on a need-to-know basis. Key external parties include major customers, Trading Standards Officers, local authorities, police (perhaps) and the media.

It may be necessary to man a crisis centre round the clock for several days, and this contingency must be taken into account. So, for example, is the petty cash float large enough to cover emergency spending? Are there enough bedrooms/bathrooms, on or near your premises, to accommodate people of both sexes for an extended period?

It is, of course, vital to keep your own staff fully informed of developments to maintain morale. At the first hint of a potential emergency, the crisis team should assemble with outside advisers to implement the prearranged plan. Ensure that all staff are trained in awareness of putative crisis situations.

Warnings could come in a variety of shapes or forms: any correspondence, fax or phone call might give valuable information of an impending crisis.

Establish lines of communication throughout the company so that relevant parties are notified and can make informed decisions.

Communications: Anticipation

Is someone in your company available to the media round the clock? Crises don't happen just during office hours. When the office is not manned, an answerphone must be used to offer an emergency number - and someone must be there to take calls. A fast response can rapidly defuse a potentially dangerous situation, but a delay in answering allows time for rumours to grow and spread. Institute a weekend/overnight rota with the duty person available at all times. If they plan to be away from their home, they must still be contactable on a mobile telephone or, at the very least, they must check using a remote device to play back the answerphone at their home or head office. The person on call will have a copy of the Action Guide which should include all the phone numbers of key personnel.

Senior personnel need to leave instructions where they can be contacted if they are away from the office: ideally, holidays will be scheduled so that all key senior personnel are not away at the same time. Again, contact numbers should be made available whenever possible.

You require a system that enables members of the crisis team and support staff to be contacted quickly. If a crisis breaks out of office hours, the person receiving the first notification of a problem must immediately contact the crisis team leader/co-ordinator, who will initiate the action plan, from home if necessary. While vital initial calls are being made by the team leader to the media and other target sources, the person receiving the original call contacts the other support team members. This could take place using a mobile phone as the duty person travels to the crisis handling centre.

The centre is the nucleus of the operation: you must have in place all the facilities you need - phones, fax machines, computers and word processors, photocopiers, a blackboard and chalks, flip-charts, stationery - to say nothing of food (no strong drinks!) and kitchen facilities and beds/bedding or rooms booked close at hand to set you up for what could be a long drawn-out incident.

Cover ancillary logistical points such as ready access to the centre for team members and support staff out of office hours (identify and brief keyholders). You and the team will need to start using the Action Guide immediately: are there enough copies? You should establish a crisis-handling area as the core of the centre, like the Incident Room in a crime investigation, with full administrative and secretarial backup. Your switchboard will already have been divided to allocate certain lines for incoming calls, others for calls out. The duty rota will list personnel to field the initial flurry of calls.

To help the co-ordinator monitor the situation, he/she will need radio and television with recording facilities. Lines of communication should be opened to key members of the trade and media. A well-briefed team will start preparing press releases and statements for approval and dispatch.

Action Plan

This is the plan your Action Guide has laid down:

- assemble the team
- chair a team meeting to assess the problem
- establish the facts and parameters for action
- assign areas of responsibility (media, trade, liaison etc, and get them working
- assign dedicated telephone/fax lines
- open a crisis/media log
- contact the media if applicable and issue holding statements
- reassure key trade customers (if appropriate)
- brief other relevant members of trade/Trading Standards Officers/police/other interested parties
- if product recall is necessary, formulate and place advertising and accompanying press releases to get your case across first
- keep the developing situation constantly under review. Not all crises become public but, if the issue breaks, capitalise on national radio/television bulletins
- probe for the issue to be broadened industry-wide to deflect the flak from your company
- check out industry/trade bodies you can look to for support.

The crisis team **must** be allowed to concentrate only on the emergency: their normal areas of responsibility will be delegated or put on hold.

Keep a log as the crisis unfolds, both for a record of all actions and calls, and to identify lessons which can be learned for the future. This chronological log should contain all actions, telephone/fax calls made or received, and all statements issued. The last point is vital in ensuring continuity and a unified company approach.

Brief the team manning the phones to prioritise them according to an agreed pattern, and pass them to the appropriate person. For instance, a call from BBC Television's main evening news slot received at 8.45pm needs answering before a call logged around the same time from News At Ten. Try to keep one fax machine in reserve for emergency messages.

It is the co-ordinator's task to brief interested parties, both internal and external. Clearly, senior executives - if they are not part of the team - must be informed so that they know what to say - and, more important, what not to say. Major trade cust-omers should know what is happening on the guarantee of strict confidentiality. It is imperative they hear of developments from you, and not through reading about them in the media or getting phone calls from journalists.

The Media

Never try to lie your way out of a crisis. You will always be found out - although you are permitted to be selective with the truth. However you choose to handle the crisis, it is imperative to have position statements and media comment available as soon as possible. Good media management is vital - and could save the day for you. Deploy your team of **trained** media spokespeople to deal with all sectors of the media, print and electronic, with the authority to speak freely on behalf of the company. Choose your spokespeople wisely: for example, if the crisis involves possible lack of product confidence you need a spokesperson who is convincing and coherent who can win back customer- and brand-loyalty.

All spokespeople must tell the same story. Any contradictions will be swooped on by journalists and lead inevitably to further problems. Crisis management is largely a media exercise, so make certain you, and not the media, are in charge.

These are inviolable ground rules for the media team:
- deceiving the press will invariably backfire on you
- do not lose your temper
- do not say "No Comment"
- use holding statements until you have something definite to say
- tell the press only what you want them to know
- always return a journalist's call
- express concern and sympathy for anyone personally/ financially affected by whatever has happened

167

- reassure people that the matter is or will be thoroughly investigated
- stress your company's excellent hygiene/safety/quality record
  ☐ **never** speculate on the cause of the problem
  ☐ **never** admit blame or negligence
  ☐ **do not** commit your company to compensation

Holding Statements

In essence, the holding statement - based on carefully constructed position statements prepared to cope with any emergency - is one which can be modified at short notice to suit a number of situations. The aim of the holding statement is to give the media/consumers enough information to answer initial queries, with the promise of more to come.

Chapter 8
APPENDIX

Media Briefing Notes

These notes summarise the advice given to you in preceding chapters. They present practical ideas on how to get publicity and develop good media relations.

Objective

Identify the objective, then plan the best way of achieving it.

Target

Aim off-target and you will waste a great deal of time and effort sending material to the wrong people, or seeing it thrown away.

Remember...

Ninety per cent of all press releases are discarded unused.

Make Use Of The Media

Supply what the media needs. You must know the functions of the key people:

- the Diary/Forward Planning Editor who will log the events you wish to publicise
- the News Editor, who will decide whether it should be covered
- the Picture Editor, who will allocate a photographer
- the Features Editor/Programme Producer, who can provide extended coverage
- correspondents who write on specialist matters
- reporters/photographers/cameramen/soundmen - the front line troops.

Develop contacts, know what they want - and give it to them.

Newspapers

National newspapers are the home for big stories:

- Use your contacts wisely and sparingly
- Do not get a reputation for over-selling - or under-supplying
- National papers use national stories: make certain yours are national stories.

Regional papers want stories about local events, local people, local companies. Their aim is simple: to sell their papers. Stories designed for this market must have:

- a strong local angle of solid interest to their readers
- a photo opportunity - pictures sell papers, especially interesting and unusual photographs
- tell the local media anything you think might be of interest
- call a local paper contact to check the news value of your story
- get the story in the editorial diaries so that there are sufficient staff on duty to cover it (news desks and picture desks often work independently of each other).

Radio

Local radio is also looking for local stories. Stations have an enormous appetite for news/current affairs stories that affect their listeners:

- Establish contacts and keep them informed
- Find out when current affairs programmes are broadcast
- Select the best spokesperson to present your case on radio
- Learn radio skills, and practice your "target" message
- Offer local radio something - or someone - of interest...
- ...you will earn their gratitude.

Television

Employ the same principles as above:

- offer good television in story and spokesperson
- trail the story in advance
- get it in the diary...
- ...leave time for scheduling space and camera crews.

Press Releases

Know the target:

- every magazine and newspaper has a theme...
- ...and a style...
- ...and a preferred size for news stories and features
- follow these leads.

It is often better to write several press releases and target them to specific outlets than to have a general release which may be of interest to few.

Follow these basic rules for press releases:

Writing:

- Avoid flowery and technical language
- Imagine you are telling a story to a friend
- Write it down in the same relaxed manner
- Don't try to be literary
- Keep sentences and paragraphs short.

A sentence should seldom be more than 25 words long - often less. Paragraphs should usually contain two or three sentences.

Concentrate on the facts

Ask yourself -

WHAT is the event about?

WHY is it being held?

WHEN is it taking place?

HOW is it being organised?

WHERE is it taking place?

WHO is involved?

HOW can they be contacted?

Remember: give contact addresses and day/evening telephone numbers.

Layout:

- double or treble spacing, on one side of the paper only
- wide margins for sub-editing and corrections
- put at the top of the page -
  - □ full name
  - □ address and organisation
  - □ day and night telephone numbers
- a short, punchy headline to encapsulate the story, or

171

- provoke enough interest to make someone read on
- never assume people know who you are and what you do
- avoid company or professional jargon and abbreviations
- use first names, not initials.

Newspapers will not be familiar with every village or small town so tie it in to a well-known location.

- use quotes - they add interest, but...
- keep them short and pithy.

Length:

Keep the press release short but make sure that all the salient points are covered. For features or articles, study the paper/journal for which you are writing. A feature of between 750 and 1,000 words is usually enough.

Pictures:

Always think of photo-angles. Pictures make news stories more interesting, sell papers, and can frequently be used by themselves with a brief caption, or a deep caption for the free-standing "picture story". Photos should be glossy black and white prints of standard size, or good quality colour prints or transparencies. Sending negatives can cause problems. Do not "pose" shots. Make them natural, but "different", and fill the frame. Type a caption and fasten it to the back of the print. Do not write on the back of the photograph itself; you will damage the front surface. Whenever possible send a choice of pictures. And if the event is big enough or spectacular enough the paper/television station will cover it themselves.

Timing:

Releases for weekly papers should arrive three or four days before publication. Those for regional dailies (morning or evening) should arrive 24 hours before the desired publication time. Monday morning papers often have quite large sections of news pages to fill, while Friday/Saturday papers are normally tight. Radio and television stations like as much warning as possible and may already be preparing programmes in which your news story could be incorporated. You might get the bonus of being invited on to the airwaves to put your story across.

PRESS CONFERENCES

These can be useful weapons for obtaining publicity but they can backfire. Points to bear in mind:

- ☐ stage a press conference only if you have a good story and someone able to put it across well
- ☐ assemble a press pack and also send it to those unable to attend
- ☐ choose the time and location carefully
- ☐ check with national/local papers to make certain your event does not clash with others
- ☐ send out a "teaser"
- ☐ tell the media the event is to be held
- ☐ give enough information to make them want to attend...
- ☐ ...but not so much that they can write it there and then
- ☐ follow this with a formal invitation at least a fortnight before the event.

It is always a challenge, and an achievement, to place your story in the media, and it is frustrating when you fail, so...

- • Ask yourself why did it fail?
- • Did it clash with a major news event?
- • If it did, remember that this is an avoidable pitfall
- • If it did not, ask yourself this:
  - ☐ was the story really good enough?
  - ☐ did you give the media sufficient notice?
  - ☐ did you target the event correctly?
  - ☐ could you have chosen a better time/location?

You will probably find that at least one of these key points let you down - but don't leave it there: the situation might still be resolved, to a degree.

Call selected news desks to find out why the story didn't land. It could, for instance, simply have gone astray in the incoming mail - in which case you are still in with a chance. Talk your way into developing the story for the paper/radio station; give them a new angle; try to sell it as a feature.

And bear in mind always that the Press Association (or Reuters, if the story is international) is of crucial importance. A newspaper which has chosen not to cover your story - or failed to through error or lack of notice/staff - will still give you publicity by picking up a persuasive agency piece.

Handling the media is not difficult if you get the basic rules right. The more professional you are in your approach, the more likely you are to put your message across successfully.

173